"I Can't Believe
I Get Paid
To Do This!"

*Remarkable People Reveal 26
Proven Strategies for Making
Your Dreams a Reality*

Stacey M

GOLD LEAF PUBLIS

Published by Gold Leaf Publishing
Post Office Box 800041
Roswell, GA 30075
www.IGetPaidToDoThis.com

Library of Congress Control Number: 2004111661

Cover/Interior Design: Jill Balkus
Editorial: The Sattinger Group
Proofreading: Precision Proofreading

Printed in the United States of America

ISBN 0-9760776-0-4

Disclaimer: The information and recommendations in the book are presented in good faith and are for general information purposes only. Every effort has been made to ensure the materials presented are accurate, that the information presented in the interviews was current and up to date at the time the interviews were conducted and the web addresses listed were active at the time of printing. This information is provided as is and no representation or warrants, either expressed or implied are made with respect to this information or any product or service referred to in this information.

All information is supplied on the condition that the reader or any other person receiving the information will do their own due diligence and make their own determination as to its suitability for any purpose prior to any use of this information.

The purpose of this book is to educate and entertain. The author, Gold Leaf Publishing and any affiliated companies shall have neither liability nor responsibility to any person or entity with respect to any loss or damage caused or alleged to have been caused, directly or indirectly, by the information contained in this book.

Contents

• • • • • • • • • •

Acknowledgments

There are numerous people I would like to thank for their help and encouragement in writing this book.

I would like to thank all my clients for they truly inspired me to write this book. Thanks to Joe Mazzeo for encouraging me to do what I do best and for the interview referrals you provided.

Thanks to Loral Langemeier, Mary Youngblood, Stacy Allison, Stephen Pierce, Tom Glavine, Dr. Van Tharp, John Dessauer, Lisa McLeod, Ricky Frank, Tedi May, Chuck Coliandro, Cynthia Zaahl, Robert Petteway, Wiley Long, Margot Swann, Carmel Anderson and Paula Rosput, for contributing your time, wisdom and experience.

Thanks to my wonderful friend, editor and encourager, Andrea Sattinger, and my transcriptionist, Barbara Morgan. Thanks for the creative input from Randy Peyser, Steve Harrison, and Susan Harrow.

Thanks to my friends and coaches, Rich Fettke and Jeanna Gabellini, who helped me in becoming the coach I am today and for your never-ending support. Thanks to my writing buddies, Gail Mills and Donna Poisl.

Thanks to everyone who gave me referrals for interviews including Alex Peers, Myra McElhaney and Susan Strevens. Thanks to my women's group for all your support–Barbara Mazzeo, Elaine Tibbitts, Myra McElhaney and Susan Saul and to everyone in my Mastermind groups and my awesome AMP group.

Thanks to Jayne Garrett, my Saturday coffee buddies and those friends who who have been avid enthusiasts from the first concept of the book.

Thanks to my husband, Mike Scruggs, who stood by me and encouraged me through this entire process. I love you.

Introduction

• • • • • • • • • • • • • • • •

This book is for the dreamers of the world; those who want more than the status quo and who know more is possible.

It is for the non-traditionalists of society; those who rebel against the rules, mores, and traditions that don't make sense to them.

It is for those with an entrepreneurial or creative spirit who want to climb to new levels of success.

It is for those who relish the idea of saying, "I Can't Believe I Get Paid To Do This!" (and for those who already say it).

And it is for the seekers of the world–those who are constantly searching....

If you are one of millions of people who have experienced success in one or more areas of your life but have other dreams that are unfulfilled, then this book is for you. Perhaps you've dreamt of writing your own book; starting a new business or taking the current one to new levels; recording your own music, performing on stage; creating residual income while you play at the beach; having your own Bed and Breakfast; investing in real estate; traveling around the world; or playing professional sports–and the list goes on and on. We all have dreams. Sometimes we suppress them or purposely squash them or we get confused about them, but we all have them.

This book is not just about achieving the dream. It is about the journey. The journey is every day of our life. If you are not enjoying the journey, then the actual achievement of the dream may give you a temporary high but leave you feeling empty inside.

To continue dreaming is what makes life exciting – it keeps it interesting. It is how we learn and grow. All of the people who I interviewed have achieved success with their dreams and they continue to have new dreams–sometimes it is another business goal, sometimes it is about having more balance in their lives or better relationships, but there is always more to learn. We are always evolving and our needs and desires change and grow as we change and grow.

So what will you get from reading this book?

You will:

1) Learn what it takes to make your dreams come true from people who have done it.

2) Receive coaching from me, The Dream Queen. As a Master Certified Coach, I will guide you in applying the key concepts in these interviews to your own life.

3) Begin to understand what we as human beings do to sabotage ourselves and start to recognize when you do these things so you can shift them.

How I selected the people to be in this book:

Many people ask me how I selected the people to be in this book. The main criterion was that they had to love what they were doing and they needed to have achieved a certain level of success at it. Some of them I intentionally sought out; many were referred to me, and most of the connections happened synchronistically. I interviewed many more people than there was actually room to include in this book. All had fabulous stories to tell and I greatly appreciate their sharing them with me. I learned something from everyone I spoke with.

When selecting the people and their stories, I wanted a diversity of topics that included many of the things that people dream about. The point is not whether you actually want to go into one of these fields as much as it is to hear the philosophies of the people of who have done these things and notice what sets them apart—what enabled them to go past fears and obstacles and actually live their dreams.

Each story that I selected has a different viewpoint, a different twist, and new things that you can learn. No two are alike. Some will resonate with you more than others; some may bring up fears or feelings of inadequacy, others excitement and delight. Your favorite story may be someone else's least favorite. Know that there is something to get from all of them. To get the most from this book, read each story with the intention to get value and you will.

I consistently tell my clients, that in virtually every profession, there are those who are struggling to get by, those who are highly successful, and those who fall somewhere in between. If you want to be one of the successful ones, then you need to learn what the successful people did to get there; that is, choose a successful artist to emulate rather than focusing on all the starving artists in the world. This book is a tool to help you do just that.

The Cast:

Stacy Allison

Stacy Allison was the first American woman to successfully climb Mt. Everest. She is also an author and speaker, and the owner of a construction company. You will hear how she balances it all and the life lessons she has learned both from climbing and from an abusive first marriage. Learn how she followed her passions and makes a great living as a result.

Mary Youngblood

From the time she was a young girl, Mary Youngblood always dreamed of being on stage and being the best at something. In 2003 she won a Grammy award for the best Native American album. You will learn how she has gone from welfare mom to Grammy Award winner and how visualizing her dream was one key to her success.

Loral Langemeier

Loral Langemeier is a financial coach, single mom, and self-made millionaire. The birth of her child made her more-rather than less-determined to succeed. Learn how she became extremely successful while keeping her relationship with her son a top priority and how learning from the best accelerated her learning curve.

Stephen Pierce

Stephen Pierce is an entrepreneur, Internet marketing specialist, and self-made millionaire whose formal education ended in the 10th grade. Stephen hit bottom and filed bankruptcy before finding his stride but he never gave up. Persistence and a willingness to learn and try new things got him where he is today.

Tom Glavine

Tom Glavine, professional ball player for the New York Mets, learned pretty early in life to bounce back from failure. He learns from his mistakes, puts them behind him, and moves on to the next situation. He also has back-up plans for most of his goals. Learn how this has helped in the attainment of his goals and how he has managed to maintain success even after his family became his number one priority.

John Dessauer

John Dessauer, real estate investor, business owner, and multi-millionaire, left his corporate job to save his broken marriage. He wanted more freedom and needed time to spend with his family. John found his niche in multi-unit real estate investing. He became a multi-millionaire in just two years *and* mended his marriage. He now once again refers to his wife as his best friend.

Lisa Earle McLeod

> Lisa Earle McLeod, humorist and author of *Forget Perfect*, got in touch with the fact that she is a very funny person and then combined that talent with her desire to help other women. She left her lucrative position at Proctor and Gamble, which was never a fit for her, despite pressure from family to stay in such a "great job." You will learn how she did it and why there is no turning back for her now.

Dr. Van K. Tharp

> Dr. Van K. Tharp, psychologist and trading coach, teaches traders how to be more successful in the stock market. In this bonus section, he shows you what we as human beings do to sabotage our dreams. Even if you are very successful, you are likely to see yourself in his examples and take away great tips for shifting old behaviors and patterns.

Key Success Principles:

Each interview is followed by three key success principles I gleaned from the conversations I had with these remarkable individuals. You will find many more success principles in each story but I chose to highlight the top three principles that were best captured by that particular story.

There are also coaching questions that coincide with each success principle. Coaching questions are questions that cause you to look inside yourself; to get in touch with your inner wisdom. These are the types of questions I ask my clients to help them move forward. Here they are meant to help you apply the concepts you learn to your own life and dreams. Following each set of coaching questions are suggested action steps. If you are inspired by a concept, it is important that you take action now while the emotion is high. Use that emotion to fuel your motivation. If you don't take action fairly soon, the sense of urgency will start to diminish. A month from now, the passion may be withering. A year from now, you may not even remember you had it. When you are inspired to take action, put the book down and go take that action. Come back to the next chapter when you are ready for more. Otherwise, you may find yourself overwhelmed with too many things to do, and that can lead to paralysis.

This book will inspire you even if you only read the interviews. But to get the most value, make the time to answer the coaching questions and then take action based on what you see for yourself. It is great to be inspired by others who are living their dreams–it is even better to be living your own dreams.

What this book is not:

I believe we all have dreams that we have suppressed and reading these stories may re-ignite some old desires that you forgot you even had. That having been said, this is *not* a step-by-step book on how to figure out what you want to do with your life.

This book is not *just* about making money. It is not *just* about doing what you are passionate about. And it is not about living your dreams to the exclusion of family and people you care about. It *is* about having what you want in all areas of your life with ease and abundance. That is what I am passionate about.

My passion and where it came from:

In 1995, I decided I wanted to help people get clear about what they wanted in life and in making it happen. Upon reaching this realization, I wondered where this passion for helping people live out their dreams stemmed from. I looked to my life for the answers and my motivation quickly became evident.

I always had the impression my dad was unhappy. Actually, miserable is more the way I would describe him. He was mostly unhappy about his jobs—all of them that I can remember. I vividly remember my father coming home from work with his shoulders hunched over and his head hanging low. He would walk right past a mosaic picture of horses pulling a carriage through the snow.

Looking exhausted and sad, he would sit down at the kitchen table and say to my mom, "Charlie (that's what he called her), I can't take it anymore. I want to quit my job!" And I can remember my mom, who was looking after our security and well-being in the best way she knew how, saying, "Just hang in there Mac. Stick it out! We need the money!" And I can remember thinking, 'Yeah! Hang in there! We need the money!' We didn't have much money in those days.

This story repeated itself year after year as my dad persevered. The last two years of his career were, for him, a countdown to retiring at age 65. Two years after he retired, he did some introspective thinking at the prompting of his daughter. At age 67, my dad declared himself an artist. I can still remember the moment he told me about it. My eyes got teary as I recalled the beautiful, mosaic picture on their living-room wall.

You see, my dad made that mosaic picture, but I never saw him working on it. He created it before I was born. It was a beautiful mosaic, made of thousands of small hand-cut tiles. My dad had always been an artist but had suppressed that talent for most of his life while he strove to earn a living for his family. He worked in the garment industry in New York, and then the carpet industry in Florida. I often wonder what would have been possible if my dad had found a way to utilize his artistic abilities in his jobs. He had always been a good employee; he might have been a happy one, too.

For a while after he retired, my dad was happier than I had ever seen him. He carved birds on wooden plaques and gave them away as gifts. He traveled to places he had never seen. He also made more money in his investments than he had at his previous jobs. I am glad he had that short time period when he was happy. Unfortunately, it wasn't too long before my dad's health started to decline. Eventually, he lost patience and could no longer focus on his artwork. Soon he was not strong enough to travel. He died at age 76.

My dad waited until he retired to do what he loved. It was a small window in the whole continuum of his life. That is why, more than ever, I strongly urge people to move forward now–don't wait until you retire to do what you love. We all tend to live as if we have forever, but really, who knows what our time allotment is? Are you doing what you love to do?

Where I am in my journey:

I have fulfilled many dreams and others are yet to be lived out. From the time I was a little girl, I wanted to have my own business–at that time I thought it would be a clothing boutique. (Actually, Dad thought I would have a clothing boutique; he even named it for me: *Len Stacey Limited*.)

Instead, I decided I wanted to make a positive impact on the lives of others. I wanted to empower people to live out their dreams with ease and abundance. In 1995 I left a successful corporate job, where I was Vice President of Human Resources, to start my business, The Center for Balanced Living. I coached my first paying client over a cup of coffee at Starbucks. Afterwards I remember thinking, *"I Can't Believe I Get Paid To Do This!"* – I get paid to talk to this interesting person…to do something that I have naturally been doing all my life. My hope and intention is that everyone who so desires will say *I Can't Believe I Get Paid To Do This* with regard to their career.

On the personal side, I left an unhealthy marriage many years ago and have since found and married my soul mate. We live on a lake with our two golden retrievers, Lover Boy and Georgia.

I have talked about writing a book for many years and now it is actually in print.

But more important than those achievements is what I learned along the way. I learned about what I wanted from a career by noticing what was missing from my career as it was. I learned how to have a healthy relationship from first having one (okay, maybe more than one) that was toxic. I am writing a book after having started two books that I did not complete. I went from doing things the hard way and working long hours by myself, to creating with ease an ongoing stream of business. I did this with the help of others and by learning to harness the universal Laws of Attraction. I now teach others how to create their careers and businesses with ease.

And I have more dreams. I am working toward lifelong goals of inner peace and financial independence. I have made significant progress on that path and I learn more every day. But if I die tomorrow, I will know that I was the creator of my own life, I experienced true unconditional love, and I made a difference in the lives of many others. For those things, I am very grateful.

The people in this book created their own lives—every success as well as every failure. It is my hope that you will learn a great deal from them and from me as you move forward to make your dreams a reality. Take what resonates with you and toss the rest. But if you find yourself resisting something, know that it may be exactly the thing you need to do to go to the next level.

I wish you the best in living out your dreams and in shouting from the rooftops, "I Can't Believe I Get Paid To Do This!"

Chapter #1:
Stacy Allison

First American Woman to Successfully Climb Mt. Everest

Adventurer Turns Her Passion into Dollars

Chapter 1

Stacy Allison
Adventurer and Business Owner
First American Woman to Successfully Climb Mt. Everest

> *"The road to happiness lies in two simple principles: find what it is that interests you and that you can do well, and when you find it, put your whole soul into it–every bit of energy and ambition and natural ability you have."*
>
> - John D. Rockefeller III, Philanthropist

I'm here today with Stacy Allison, mountain climber extraordinaire. Stacy is the first American woman to successfully climb Mt. Everest. She is also a speaker, an author and owner of a construction company, and is married with two sons.

Let's just start with the mountain climbing because that's not something that everyone does every day. When did you start mountain climbing and how did you choose to do that?

Well, I didn't actually choose to do it; I sort of fell into it. In my first year of college at Oregon State University, I had an opportunity to go down to Zion National Park in Southern Utah to go rock climbing. Basically a fellow put a notice on the bulletin board in my dorm, saying that he was going down there, and he wanted to share a ride with someone. And so, another girlfriend and I decided this sounded like a great adventure. Neither of us had climbed before. We went down there and Kurt was this fellow's name, Kurt showed us the very basics of climbing sheer rock cliffs. And, of course, at the age of 19, I stood down at the bottom watching him climb up, and, he made it look so easy–like ballet on a vertical plane. And I thought to myself, well, hmm, I could do that.

But it was much more difficult than I had ever anticipated. I got on that rock and I slowly climbed up while falling numerous times and whining, "Let me down, let me down." Forty-five minutes later, I made it to the top and it was a feeling of exhilaration that I had never felt before. I could hardly wait to go down and try again. It was almost immediately that I knew this was what I was meant to do, that this was it.

Say more about the feeling of exhilaration. Tell us what that felt like and what went through your mind then.

It's emotional. It's not intellectual. It's a rise of energy and emotion that basically starts in your toes and works its way up through at least, what it did for me, you know, up through my body. And it was the excitement, the realization that, I can do this, I can do this. I mean, it was tough, it was really hard for me, but I also knew that mentally I had what it took, if I chose to do this. And when I say passion; that was almost immediate. I don't know how to explain that to people, and people will often say, well, how could it be immediate? I'm not sure I can tell you how I knew that, but climbing is where my spirit soars. When I am climbing, whether it's a sheer rock cliff or a mountain, I belong in no other place. I am absolutely where I should be. It's where I feel the most connected to this Earth and the most at peace, even if I'm in an absolutely dangerous challenging situation.

It's amazing to hear that because it seems like it would be the opposite, but obviously you feel very connected.

Yes. And, you know, I am very spiritual and I believe that there is a universal energy that flows through everything, and when I'm climbing, that energy is flowing from the mountain, from the rock to me, back to the rock, back to the mountain. So it's a give-and-take kind of energy; I don't conquer a mountain, a mountain is kind enough to let me climb on it for a very brief time.

So you knew after that first time that you were going to be doing more of this?

I knew I was going to be doing more so I actually climbed throughout the summer and learned rock climbing. I started out climbing rock cliffs. And then that winter I actually went mountain climbing for my first time and, of course, I never do anything the easy way. I went with a couple of friends who had been climbing for at least ten years to do a winter ascent of a very small mountain here in Oregon. But we did a winter blizzard ascent of this mountain, and I remember my hands being so cold that I was in tears. It was a long, grueling day. It took us probably 18 hours to ski in, to climb the mountain, and we skied back out around midnight. I was so exhausted that I knew if I had fallen over on my skis I wouldn't have been able to get up.

But what I learned on that trip is how I indeed had the mental capacity to push myself far beyond what I was capable of doing, and I knew, and I understood that that's what it took if I wanted to climb mountains. And it fascinated me; I mean the mental aspect of climbing is what truly fascinates me.

Oh, interesting because I would have thought the opposite. I would have thought the physical is what most people do it for.

Well, certainly the physical is a good way to stay healthy and in shape and all that, but really it's the mental aspect. Because when you're hanging off a rock cliff you have to be holding onto the rock, but if you're holding on too tight, you're going to exhaust yourself, and so it's a mental game. How can I conserve my energy without falling off the rock? When it takes 20 days to climb a mountain, you've got to be able to conserve your energy. You've got to be able to push yourself far beyond just the next step. So it's very mental.

So you really have to be thinking through your strategy the whole way and constantly stay focused?

Yes. Absolutely. The only time you can let up is when you're in your tent for the night. I mean there are times if you're doing something easy where you can let up your focus. But really you've got to be able to focus for hours and hours and hours. And, at the same time, for example, when we're climbing Mt. Everest, it took me 29 days from the base of the mountain, before I actually stood on top. Now, I'm not climbing every single day of those 29 days. It's just like in our job; if we don't take a break, we burn out. And so it's very important to, even though you have to work many days in a row, that you also back off and take a break, mentally and physically, so that you can come back with renewed energy, perhaps with a different perspective.

I can hear the analogy to climbing a mountain and attaining any other goal in life. If you hold on too tight to anything, it's not going to happen.

Well, our perspectives become skewed anytime you hold on too tight. When you cannot back off and look at it from a different perspective, from a more objective point of view; if you get so emotionally, mentally, physically, wrapped up in your work and your way of doing whatever it is you're doing, you tend to be wearing blinders, and you need to be able to back off, let up that energy, to get perspective.

Right. So what would you say has been your greatest challenge in mountain climbing, per se?

Oh, I thought you were going to ask me my greatest challenge in life.

Well we can go there if you want.

That would be raising my two sons. That's a climb that never lets up.

My biggest challenge to date, climbing, was actually when I climbed Mt. McKinley-Denali in Alaska. And the reason that was the greatest challenge is because of the experience and skill level I had at the time. I climbed one of the most difficult routes on the mountain, and I had only been climbing for about three and a half years. That's relatively little experience. I was a very good climber, but it was definitely an eye-opener, and that was the most challenging.

So, you took on something that was a little bit beyond your experience at that point?

Yes. And actually, I must say I've always done that in climbing, and I do that in many things in my life. I was raised with parents who encouraged their children to pursue their interests, to pursue whatever it was that interested them. And, it was OK if we made mistakes as long as we learned from those mistakes. And so I'm a risk taker and I think it's because of that. I'm not afraid to fail, to make blunders, and I've always had a supportive group of friends and family who have allowed me to do that. And, in climbing, I started climbing with people who had 10, 15 years of experience climbing, and they allowed me to go on mountains, on rock climbs, that I really wasn't prepared for, yet they knew I would learn a lot and it was OK with them.

So I wasn't depending on myself to get myself through situations I knew nothing about. They were there to help with that, and I must say my learning curve was huge. As I mentioned on Denali, I went with someone who had been climbing for at least 15 years, and even though I pulled my own weight, he was there to mentor me along the way.

That leads into the next question, which was about who your mentors and role models have been. It sounds like you've chosen to go on these trips with people with a lot more expertise than you, at least in the beginning?

In the beginning, absolutely. And, again, I feel very fortunate that I had the opportunity to do that, because in a matter of four, five years, I was actually doing it. I didn't have to depend on those people who had been climbing for those many years. I could actually depend on myself and take people who were less experienced or equally experienced.

You said you felt fortunate to be able to climb with those people who had a lot of expertise early on. Well, did they just say, "Hey, Stacy, come on with us," or did you ask them?

It worked both ways. I think I showed talent so they were interested. You know, again, I guess maybe part of it goes back to this mental capacity, pushing myself far beyond what I think I'm capable of doing. Certainly I've pulled my weight. I would pull my weight, and so they were very encouraging. But I just have been very fortunate to have friends who aren't so concerned with achieving the top of the mountain as they are with having fun, with taking new people out and showing them how to do things, and helping other people succeed. I mean it's a give-and-take.

And I feel, for example, in my construction business, I do the same thing. I am thrilled to be able to mentor young people who have no experience. It's important; it's terribly important.

I want to come back to the construction business in a minute. But first, you were climbing all these mountains and one thing that I want to ask you is, where did you find the time? It sounds like mountain climbing is very time-consuming. I mean, you have to be in shape, and they're not short jaunts, so where did you find the time to make all these mountain climbing trips happen?

Well, what I did was I worked odd jobs here and there. I would work for three months, get enough money to go off and do a climb, then I'd come back and I'd work until I got enough money to go off and do another climb. But then I have to say that I actually did get married, and my first husband was an architect and builder and that's how I actually got into the construction business. And, of course, when you own your own company, it allows you the freedom to work on a project, and then you can take off and do the climbing.

But initially it sounds like climbing was a priority and you set out to make the money so you could do the climbs?

That's right. Climbing was priority. I worked so that I could climb, and that was my life. That was what I was focused on and interested in.

And I truly believe if you're going after a dream or a goal, you're always going to give up something. I don't like to use the word sacrifice, but you do have to give up something in order to gain something else.

And so you chose not to have a fully entrenched career at that time?

Oh, I wasn't interested in that at all. Because you can always work. And you may not always be able to climb mountains. Now, of course my life has changed since then, and we can talk about that.

Yes we will, definitely. All right, so, you climbed mountains pretty much as a focus for how many years, Stacy?

Oh, for probably six years. For six years, that was my sole focus.

And then you got married and you got involved in your husband's business?

Yes. And my first husband was a climber, and so we would do a project and then we would climb. Plus, I lived in Zion, just outside of Zion National Park in Southern Utah. And so we could finish the day and then go out and climb rock cliffs right in our backyard. Basically we lived there so that we could climb.

So you chose where you lived?

Absolutely, and you know, everybody has that kind of choice, no matter what career, profession, dream they choose for themselves. We all can choose where we wish to live.

And then we were married for four and a half years, and then we did divorce, and I moved from Utah back to Portland, Oregon, which is where I'm from.

Apparently you took to the construction industry as well, because I know you've started your own construction company.

Yes. I loved building. I mean, it's another love of mine. I knew that I wanted to continue building, so when I moved back to Oregon after the divorce, I started my own company.

What do you love about building?

Well, I primarily do only older homes, so I buy my projects. We end up gutting the house, which means taking the entire lathe plaster, woodwork, everything out of the house and starting from the bare bones. And then we rebuild the house in its original integrity except we add modern amenities like copper plumbing, and wiring, and things like that. I love taking something that looks like it should be bulldozed and bringing it back to life. Older homes have spirits. They've been lived in for a long time–a number of years–and they tend to have the energy and spirit of the people who have lived there. I enjoy bringing something back to life, and making something beautiful.

So a lot about the aesthetics there as well as the physical rebuilding.

Yes. And again, having my own business allows me the freedom to pursue my other activities.

I heard the passion in your voice when you spoke about it, and it also fit for you, in terms of the lifestyle you wanted to live and being able to pursue your mountain climbing and other interests?

Yes. And again, it boils down to choice.

What I hear is you made some very conscious choices and they were in alignment with your passions.

Yes, but I must also say that I was not successful at every single thing I did. My life actually has been very convoluted. I've had a lot of dips, turns, valleys and mountain peaks. I went through some pretty rough knocks to get to where I am today.

Tell us about a couple of the obstacles that you've had to overcome to get where you are.

OK. Well, let's certainly start out with my first marriage which was an abusive relationship. And people look at me today and say, "I can't believe it." Well, it happens, and it happens to many people, and that was certainly a valley in my life. But I didn't stay stuck in that valley. I must say that I learned a lot from that relationship. And…

What did you learn, Stacy?

Well, I learned that sometimes our strengths can be our weaknesses. I was an incredibly mentally strong person, and that was actually one of my weaknesses. I thought I could overcome this. I thought I could deal with it. You know, I thought I could handle that.

I CAN'T BELIEVE . . .

But we can't. I mean, nobody deserves to live in an abusive relationship.

Right.

I learned how to...how do I say this...be more selective in who my next husband would be, and I am currently married to my final husband, the father of my two children, who is very kind, very caring, very supportive. It made me smarter in choosing a lifelong partner.

And, I think it made me more compassionate. I think before that relationship, I wouldn't have had patience for a woman who is in an abusive relationship, because I didn't understand it. Now I am certainly more compassionate. I understand it. I understand when people are stuck in ruts and can't seem to get out, and it's OK that we go through hard times, that we have difficulties, and so, yes, I'm more compassionate.

So that was a pretty deep valley there, and I love what you said about your strengths, because what I heard you say earlier is one of the things that you tend to do is take on things that are beyond your capacity and you live into it, and this is one that you took on that was beyond your capacity, and you couldn't do anything about it.

Right. And you know, I'll tell you something else I learned, because this divorce happened right before my first trip to Mt. Everest. My ex-husband and I were both invited to go on the first climb, and then he was asked not to come. I went on that first climb and I thought, oh, the fame, the fortune. I'm going to show the world I'm somebody by being the first American woman to climb to the top. And I didn't make it to the top that trip. I came home empty-handed, the same Stacy Allison as before, and I was very disappointed. Certainly I had failed on other mountains before, but this had a much greater meaning because I thought it would fix everything.

When I went through my divorce, my self-esteem was virtually nonexistent. I thought I was ugly and stupid, and nobody would ever love me again. And so, I thought the top of the mountain, if I was first that would change everything. And so another big lesson I learned is that our external achievements do not change the way we think and feel about ourselves. It's not what builds self-esteem. Self-esteem is built from within, and what external achievements do for us is they help build self-confidence, which is quite a bit different from self-esteem.

It's great the distinction you're making. Say more about how you have built your self-esteem, if it wasn't from mountain climbing.

Well, I think part of it is from mountain climbing, because I do climb and what happened on that first Everest trip is that I tricked myself into thinking that the only thing that was important on this climb was reaching the summit, and being first. And so I was solely focused on the summit, and I completely missed the climb. But climbing, the act of climbing helps build self-esteem. Does that make sense? It's not whether you reach the top or not, it's the process of doing it.

Yes, I get it. So you're talking about the difference between the journey and the destination.

The destination. Exactly, exactly.

It's the journey that builds self-esteem, not the destination.

Not the destination.

Because it's on the journey that we learn about ourselves and we learn about others. And what I've noticed about climbing is you can't hide behind a three-piece suit. You can't hide behind your big mahogany desk. You come face to face with yourself. It's such an incredibly stressful environment, that you can't hide. And it gives you an opportunity, if you're open to it, to really learn about yourself, and then change those things that you don't like.

And that's the key, isn't it?

That is the key.

It's not just about looking at yourself and saying "Yuck, bad me."

Right. Or I don't like that; I don't want to be that way anymore.

Right, instead you can say, I don't like that and I'm going to change it.

Yes. Yes.

How have you used the knowledge from mountain climbing and the lessons you've learned in your construction company?

Well, as the owner...as the boss, what I understand is the importance of teamwork, and what I mean by that is on a construction site, if you come into a construction site that is run by my crew and me, we are very polite to one another. We always say please and thank you, and sub-contractors know when they're on my site because they hear that please, thank you. Before we start a project, we go through the project, we look at it, we talk about it, and we talk about the possibilities. If we're working on a project for a client, I am open to my crew talking with the client. I don't want to be the only one talking to the client; everybody needs to talk to the client because this is usually the most important investment the client will make. And, we work together, and I'll tell you, if I have a crew member who's not working as part of the team, who's not communicating, and who's not accountable and sharing responsibilities, they're not on my crew for very long. All it takes is one person who's not a team member to bring down the entire team, and I've learned that from mountain climbing.

Among some of the leadership lessons I've learned, a big one is not to blame anyone on my crew when mistakes are made. Mistakes happen in climbing, and gosh, you can't focus on the problem, you have to focus on the solution. You not only focus on the solution, but you bring everyone together to help focus on that solution, to get the buy in, so we don't blame on my crew. If mistakes are made, and boy, we've had some big mistakes–had a roof once that was put on wrong.

There's a big one.

That's a big, expensive mistake, and it took all I had not to blame. I mean, I had to bite my tongue, and I quickly threw it back at the crew, "OK, we've got a problem here, how are we going to fix it?" And, I didn't blame the lead carpenter. And, I'll tell you, that crew, they pulled together and they went out, and they did what they had to do to fix the roof, and then the lead carpenter came up to me afterwards and thanked me for not pointing him out and blaming him in front of everybody else. I learned that through climbing.

Has he turned out to be a good employee for you?

Absolutely, the best. You know, you treat people well, and they will treat you well.

And, it's about relationships. Gosh, I can't think of anything we do in this life that's not about relationships.

So you've learned that in mountain climbing, and you've brought it to your business, and then how did it evolve so that you started speaking and writing about it?

Once I reached the top of Mt. Everest, people started calling me, companies started calling me and asking me if I would come in and talk to their organizations. I didn't have any speaking experience at all. I had never spoken in front of anyone, and I, oh gosh, I have fallen flat on my face in speaking, but what happens to me, and I notice actually the same thing happens when I climb mountains, is that when I fall flat on my face speaking, I just want to hang my head in humiliation. However, once I get over that initial feeling of humiliation, I'm very excited because I can see what I need to do the next time, in order to be successful. Then I can see what I need to do, what I need to work on, what I need to practice to get better.

It almost sounds like it's the way you learn, that you go ahead and you bite off more than you can chew, and you try it.

Well, that's one way to do it, and that is my way, and I certainly don't recommend that to everybody, but it works for me. I am not afraid to fall flat on my face. I'm not afraid to be laughed at, to be whatever, it doesn't really matter to me, as long as I learn, and I mean, it's very exciting.

Do you like speaking now?

I love speaking and let me tell you, I am so much better. I actually love it, and I have learned…the learning curve, again, has been tremendous, and I feel so fortunate that I am able to do this.

How long has it taken you, would you say, to go from falling flat on your face to being confident as a speaker?

Well, I started speaking in probably 1990, although not seriously, I would just do it here and there when people called me. But I've been seriously speaking for the last six years, and I am not falling flat on my face anymore. So I would say from maybe the first four years, five years that I first started speaking where I would just dabble in it, where I would not commit. You see, it's a lot easier when you don't because if you fall flat on your face, you sort of have an excuse, "Well, I wasn't serious about that, anyway."

Yes, very good point.

Yes, but once I committed six years ago, I won't let myself fall flat on my face. I mean, I am prepared, I do my research, and I'm ready.

There's a big difference. I really want to reiterate the difference in how you perform when you're just kind of going along and doing it as it comes up versus when you're committed to something.

That's right, because when you're committed, again, you only have yourself to fall back on. You are accountable for your performance, and it's just like in climbing mountains, once you commit, you don't have anybody else to blame but yourself, for your performance. It's like it is in everything.

You've also written a couple of books.

I have. I actually had an agent who contacted me and said, "Oh, you must write a book about your Everest experience."

That pinnacle opened a lot of doors for you.

Yeah, it certainly did, and I said, "I'm not a writer," and they said, "That's OK, we'll find a writer to work with you." So the first book was actually co-written, and then the second book I did by myself.

So, yes, climbing Everest opened a lot of doors, and you know, that's the exciting thing. Sometimes people say, "Well, I've got this opportunity but in order to take advantage of that opportunity, I'll have to maybe give up my job, and I'm not sure, what if this opportunity doesn't work out?" It's that waffling, but once you go for that opportunity, I mean, the doors open, and the world is out there, ready for us to take advantage of it and to utilize it.

And what I really hear Stacy, is you followed your passions, you made them a priority, and while it hasn't always been easy, it has paid off for you.

It has and I must also say that I have two young sons now, and I am no longer climbing big, dangerous mountains.

Now, again, this was a choice. I chose to have children, and my responsibility now is to my children. It is not for Stacy Allison to go out and pursue her dreams. My priorities have shifted. My responsibility now is to raise kind, caring, healthy young men, and someday I will go back to climbing big, dangerous mountains, but not right now.

How do you balance mountain climbing, owning your own company, being an author, being a speaker, and having two kids? I mean, that's a lot.

Yes, it boils down to priorities. My first and number one priority are my children and I only speak 50 times a year. When I'm done with my 50, I'm done. If I spoke more than that, I wouldn't have time for my family, and they need me. Right now I am not working for clients in my construction company. I am buying my own projects, so the timeline is strictly my timeline.

I have, as I mentioned before, a very supportive husband. This is my time, so to speak, career-wise, in that speaking is available to me. I will not always want to speak, and I know this so, again, it's a choice that I'm making. I'm speaking now, but when I reach a certain age, I'm not going to want to speak, so now is my time, and pretty soon, it's going to be David's time to then get back into his career. My husband is a physician. So, he's put his career, not on hold, he's actually doing exactly what he wants to do, but he's only working part-time so that I can pursue my dreams and goals.

So your husband does some of the taking care of the family while you're out speaking.

Absolutely. I couldn't do it if he was not here to help with that. I wouldn't want to do it. Let's put it that way.

Again, I hear your priorities are very clear, and you and your husband have found ways that work for both of you so you can do your speaking and make sure that your kids' needs are met.

I CAN'T BELIEVE . . .

Yes.

And, I love what you said about how you are only taking on projects again that work with your timeline.

Right, right, and you know, it's not about the money, and I think that people need to be real clear about that, too. Why it is that you're pursuing whatever it is that you're pursuing. If it's about the money, then I don't truly believe you can have passion around money. I believe it has to come from what it is you're doing, and so, the money part has never been important to us. It's pursuing the career, the job, the climbing, that type of thing that's important.

You certainly didn't start climbing mountains for the money.

Oh gosh, no.

But, in pursuing your passion, my guess is that you're done pretty well financially as a result of speaking and some of the other things you've done.

Yes, that is correct.

So, it's not that you turn away money, it's not that you don't want the money, it's that it wasn't your primary motivator for what you've done.

No. Money, simply put, allows us the freedom to pursue the things that are important to us, and we've made very wise investments and things like that, so yes.

So you've used money as a tool to have what you want and to live the way you want.

Yes.

What advice do you have for anyone who has a dream, which is not yet a reality? What's one thing you would say to them?

Well, I think people need to be real clear as to why they're choosing that dream. They have to know why they want it, and sometimes, we hear all sorts of advice, and I really believe that until you're ready to act on a dream, to take the first step in pursuing, to actually reaching that dream, that you keep it to yourself. I think that when you spread it around, it really dilutes the dream. Until I was ready to climb Mt. Everest, until I actually got on an expedition and was ready to do it, I didn't tell a soul. I pursued it, you know, I applied for permits and did everything I needed to do, but I didn't tell anybody.

And how do you think that helped you?

I think it built up energy and momentum. If you start telling people and they don't believe that you can do it, those negative people will have an impact on you.

Yes, I call them dream squashers.

There you go–dream squashers–absolutely. But once you've started down your path to your dream, then you can start telling people, and once you're clear, absolutely crystal clear as to why you want it, where you're headed, those dream squashers won't be able to squash you.

That's right.

And the other thing is that people need to understand that when you set out to pursue your dream, it's not one straight line. It's going to be peaks and valleys, dips and turns, all of that, and you have to, again, be crystal clear as to what you want.

You've talked about commitment and you've talked about clarity, and do you think those two things are also what help you get past the obstacles and the valleys and those things when they come up?

Oh yes, yes, if you're not committed, if you're just out there halfheartedly… well, first of all, I just don't think you're ever going to make it. I mean you've got to be absolutely committed because that's how you hold yourself accountable. When you're committed, that's what gives you your vision, your clarity.

It's what motivates you to get up when you've been knocked down and all that.

Do you actually visualize and see yourself reaching certain goals?

Oh yes, I do. I'm a huge visualizer and I kind of call it daydreaming. But I did that on Mt. Everest, and I do that on a number of climbs that I've been on. I visualize myself at base camp, climbing the mountain, reaching the top and then, of course, you have to make it down safe or it doesn't count. And, I've done that with other things. I do that with personal relationships and with my speaking.

I think it's very beneficial to be able to visualize and see what it is you want, and not only what you want but also what it's like before you even get there.

So, to actually feel like what it would be like to have attained that.

Yes, exactly.

Great advice. We need to start to wind up, Stacy I want people to know how to find out more about you and your books, so you have a Website, right?

I do, and that is www.BeyondTheLimits.com.

And, what are the names of your books?

My first book is *Beyond The Limits, A Woman's Triumph On Everest,* and the second book is *Many Mountains To Climb–Reflections On Competence, Courage, And Commitment.*

Great, they sound wonderful. Stacy, thank you so much for sharing this with us. There are lots of lessons that you've learned along the way, and hopefully, people will take these to heart as they go forward to pursue their dreams.

I appreciate the opportunity to share with your readers and I just wish each and every one of them the very, very best as they pursue their dreams.

Three Key Success Principles Plus Coaching Questions and Action Steps

• •

Stacy Allison

Key Success Principle #1:

Honor Numero Uno: Design Your Life Around Your Priorities

Many people try to fit their dreams into their life and then complain that there are not enough hours in the day to make it happen. If you want your dream to become a reality, you have to make it a priority. Otherwise, it will never be more than a pipedream.

I am not suggesting that you become single focused on your dream to the exclusion of your family, friends or health. There are other priorities in life that are as important or often more important than your career dreams. It is important to learn to balance these things. Decide what your priorities are and live your life accordingly. Your priorities are based on what you value in life and your values will likely change over time, so it is a good idea to reassess every few years as well as any time you make a major life change.

The importance of this cannot be understated. After completing a values clarification exercise many years ago, I realized my 'ladder was leaning against the wrong wall.' That realization led me to rearrange my priorities and refocus on my relationships. It was also the impetus for launching my company, the Center for Balanced Living.

How Stacy Designs Her Life Around Her Priorities:

Stacy made a decision to focus on climbing. She initially chose to work short-term jobs to pay the bills so she could be free to climb. She also moved to an area that was conducive to climbing. Later she became an entrepreneur in a field she loved so she could have the flexibility in her schedule to climb. She made very conscious choices in alignment with her passion.

Over time Stacy's priorities changed. She had a family and her children became the most important thing to her, so she put dangerous mountain-climbing activities on the back burner for a while. She and her husband have worked out a way that allows her to pursue her speaking career while he stays home with the kids. They continue to create ways to have what they want and keep their priorities in focus.

Coaching Questions:

1) What are your highest values?

If you are unsure of what your values are or would like to reassess your values, go to the Resource Section for instructions on downloading the values assessment from my Web site.

2) How can you create your life to fit with your priorities rather than vice versa?

Call to Action:

1) Decide on three steps that will move your life in closer alignment with your priorities. Write them down.

Examples: Decide to move closer to your job so you don't have to spend so much time commuting and can spend more time with your family; have a date with your spouse every week; spend 15 minutes a day reading something about the area in which you want to excel, etc.

2) Choose to move forward with one of these steps over the next week.

Key Success Principle #2

Self-Confidence Is Built by Experience—
One Step at a Time

Having supported thousands of people in living out their dreams over the past eight years, I have noticed that one of the main things that stops people from bringing their dreams to fruition is a lack of confidence.

When you are confident, you know you will handle whatever comes up in the best way you can and move on. Regardless of what happens, you will still be whole and complete unto yourself. Confidence also means knowing that we were all born with the same inherent worth and that doesn't change based on income, status, or what others might say.

Many times people think that they need to wait and start living their dreams when they are more self-confident or feel better about themselves. It generally doesn't work that way. When you commit to a big dream, old issues that are unresolved will come up to be worked through so that you can be the type of person who can make that dream happen. Get support from a coach or mentor in dealing with perceived obstacles as they arise. Start by taking small steps. As you begin to have small successes and work past obstacles, you will become more and more confident.

How Stacy Built Her Self-Confidence and Self-Esteem:

On the first trip to Mt. Everest, Stacy focused on the fame and fortune of being the first woman to climb Mt. Everest. She thought it would change everything. She did not make it to the top on the first trip but she learned from that trip and from other things that happened in her life. She made changes accordingly and was successful on her second attempt. She learned that external achievements do not change how we think and feel about ourselves. Self-confidence comes from achieving things but self-esteem comes from within. Stacy says, "The process of doing it and learning what works and doesn't, what you do and don't like about yourself, and changing the things that you don't like is what builds self-esteem."

Often we want to take the shortcuts to reach our destination. It is important to remember that the valuable growth and learning comes from the journey and all that it provides. Ninety-five percent of our life is the journey; we might as well enjoy it.

Coaching Questions:

1) Where in life are you getting impatient because you are not as far along as you think you should be?

2) Take a look back at what you *have* done.

What steps have you taken?

What have you learned?

Where have you grown?

What obstacles have you overcome?

Call to Action:

1) On a separate piece of paper, write a list of all your accomplishments as far back as you can remember–include all the small things that seemed big at the time. Step back and allow yourself to feel good about your accomplishments.

2) Write up an infomercial about yourself for your eyes only. Introduce yourself to you and the rest of the world, emphasizing all the qualities you possess and the things you've done that make you great. Read it to yourself in the mirror every day. Own your greatness! Visualize yourself being that person in your infomercial and notice what it feels like to be that person. Then step into that visualization. Reading your infomercial is especially helpful before important meetings or events. (Use a separate piece of paper for this excercise and keep your infomercial somewhere you will see it everyday.)

Key Success Principle #3

Why Be Rich and Miserable When You Can Be Rich and Happy?

Create Money in Alignment with Your Passion

It is important to focus on what you are passionate about first and then find a way to make money at it. Get in touch with your heart first; otherwise, the left side of your brain (the logical side) will rule out perfectly good ideas without having explored them.

I have worked with a multitude of clients over the years who were unhappy in their careers and wanted to make a change. Many of those people chose their initial career chiefly because they thought it was a stable field and they could make a good living at it. I've talked to many accountants and lawyers, for example, who chose their career for this reason but ended up miserable because it wasn't a fit for their passions, talents or personalities. In recent years, many people chose the Information Technology field for this reason. These are all perfectly good careers if doing them lights you up. But if you are working at them only for the money, you may find yourself dissatisfied. If you want to do something you love and make good money too, take a stand for having both. Create a "must have" list of all the attributes you think are essential in your ideal career. Don't settle for less.

How Stacy Focused on Her Passion:

Stacy is passionate about all that she does. She says, "Passion comes from doing what you love, not from focusing on money. Money allows us the freedom to pursue the things that are important to us. Money is a tool, not an end in itself." Stacy pursued her passion for mountain climbing. As a result, she ended up being offered speaking engagements and several book contracts and is now making a good living. Her higher self knew that being the first woman to climb Mt. Everest would lead to good things and she ventured down that road and made it happen.

Coaching Question:

1) Is there something you love to do that you are not doing because you can't see how you could make money doing it? If so, what is it?

Call to Action:

1) Start doing what you love to do outside of work hours just because you love it.

2) Find people who are doing what you love to do and making money at it. Contact them and ask for an informational interview so you can learn how they did it.

People love to help; so don't be afraid to ask for a short amount of their time.

My Key Learnings from This Chapter:

1)

2)

3)

Chapter #2:
Mary Youngblood

From Welfare Mom to
Grammy Award Winner

*Musician Finds "Her Instrument"
Later in Life and Visualizes Her Way
to the Grammy*

Chapter 2

Mary Youngblood
Native American Flutist and
Grammy Award Winner

"Commitment is a line you must cross... it is the difference between dreaming and doing."

- Bernie Fuchs

I'm here today with Mary Youngblood. Mary is a Grammy Award winner, a Native American flutist, and a single mom who worked her way up from being on welfare.

How does it feel to be introduced as a Grammy Award winner?

It's really an honor. You know, I can't say enough about it. Everyone who's gotten a Grammy, or been nominated for one, says it's just absolutely an honor, but it absolutely is.

You've dreamed of this honor for a long time, haven't you?

I have, I have.

So let's go back in time, because you've made a lot of dreams happen. This Grammy was the latest of them. But, when did you start playing the flute?

I've been playing the classical flute since I was 10. It just seemed to be a natural progression, since I had played that instrument for so long, that I later picked up the Native American flute. I did that about 11 or 12 years ago.

You started out playing the classical flute and taking traditional lessons. Was that something you really loved, too?

When I first picked up the instrument, we had moved from Seattle, Washington to Tucson, Arizona, so my father could complete his dissertation. We came in mid-year, and I was in fourth grade. I really wanted to join the band but there were no instruments left by that time. All that was left to play was the classical flute, which no one wanted to play because it's a difficult instrument to learn, especially when you're 10. I said, "I don't care, I'll play any instrument. I just want to be in the band."

In an attempt to get me caught up to speed, because I had just arrived in mid-year, my parents got me some private lessons from a master's degree student at the University of Arizona in Tucson. So I kind of fell into the flute, years and years ago, because I just wanted to make music and be in the band. The flute actually chose me.

But you knew you wanted to make music. What else did you dream of when you were a little girl?

I always watched the Super Bowl, Wimbledon, the Miss America Pageant, the Olympics, anything that was the crème de la crème, where people were getting acknowledgment for being the best at something. I was drawn to those kinds of shows. I don't know exactly where that stemmed from in my child psyche. It might have something to do with having been adopted and feeling like I didn't have much of a voice as a child, and wanting some attention. I mean, who knows, but I was really drawn to those kinds of programs and events.

I would think, "Oh, it would be nice to be on stage. Wouldn't it be fun to hear the applause? Wouldn't it be great to get noticed for being the best at something?" I always wanted to be the best at something and really worked hard to achieve that. It ended up being a music career.

You knew you wanted to be the best at something. You knew you wanted to be performing. You knew you wanted to be on stage and receive that acknowledgement. And there you were just receiving that acknowledgement on the Grammy stage, so you definitely made that dream come true.

It was surreal.

I bet. It says something for dreaming and I really want to acknowledge that. Many times people put down dreams as being unrealistic and it's all up to you whether it's realistic or not, isn't it?

I really visualized it, too, even as a child watching those programs. I could visualize myself walking up the stage, up the stairs. For me, visualizing those dreams happening was pertinent to making that happen, because I could see it. I pictured it in my head.

I had an imagination, and I could just picture things—such as being at home plate at the World Series, even though, of course, I've never played baseball. But I could picture being there. I could picture playing that final wondrous winning game.

I think what you're saying is relevant for everyone. There's a saying that if you can see it, you can make it happen. That's how many athletes practice their shots. For example, golfers and tennis players visualize hitting the ball beforehand. That's what you did and that's relevant for everything in our lives. But there were some obstacles that came up along the way, weren't there?

Just a few.

Did your parents support you in this dream?

I think as well as they could, they did. For them, coming from academia, their idea of being a musician was very different from where I was headed. Their idea of that was to practice my flute for four hours a day and hope to get into Juilliard and perhaps perform in a symphony or in some kind of symphonic group.

I think for them, my having come down this avenue didn't quite fit their criteria of what being a musician was.

They had a different path in mind.

Absolutely. They had a different dream or goal for me.

They were worried, as most parents would be, about their child delving into a field that was so highly competitive and so precarious. It's feast or famine in this business. I think that they were worried for their child getting her hopes up and failing, or not quite making the grade. It's a tough business.

That seems like a natural reaction for parents to have. How did you deal with that along the way?

That was difficult. I've heard folks in front of audiences when they've won awards and they say, "I could have not have done this without my parents, I could have not have done this without my family." My friend, Rita Coolidge, said that, when I presented her with the First American Indian in the Arts Award in L.A. a couple years ago. I, on the other hand say, "I could not have done this without my children. They have been my source of strength." It's difficult when you don't feel you've had people who have always been there for you and been supportive.

You did it anyway, and I think that's important for people to see.

I didn't let anyone or anything keep me from that dream. Even if it was their best intentions to be concerned about my having that dream, I did not let that stop me. I think I became more determined, as a matter of fact. I said, "I'm going to show you." There was a little bit of that in there. I think there is with any artist who has high expectations or dreams for their career. You say, "I'm just going to do this no matter what."

Are your parents happy for you now?

Absolutely, absolutely.

You were adopted, is that correct?

I was adopted at seven months old. I began searching for my natural mother, my birth mother, in 1983 and found her in 1986. We continue to have a friendship, and I've become very, very close to one of my half sisters, Hannah. Everyone is still up in the Seattle area.

I recall your saying you were a Native American with a white family. What kind of impact did that have on you?

It was really challenging growing up being brown in a white world. I think, even now, my parents would say that they agree that most Native children should be adopted by Native parents. Of course, we're talking 1957, 1958, post-Korean War, when so many families, especially Catholic families like mine, were adopting Korean children. That was huge then. At the time it was kind of the norm, and it was done all the time. I think now we're a little bit more considerate in thinking about this child's culture, the input that that will play on their lives.
We're talking a long time ago, and it was difficult. There were times when it was challenging because I was in predominantly white neighborhoods and so I was very different. I was always aware of that, and it was something that I always understood from a very young age. There was something different about me. I had to find that place, come home, as it were, to my people, to my culture, which I feel I've done full circle.

Did you always know you were Native American or did you not know what was different?

I knew. They knew that my mother was Aleut. In fact, being raised by educators, of course we went to the library a lot and looked at books. There weren't a lot on the Aleut people, but we tried to find what we could on Native American people so that I would have some kind of information about my heritage, which was pretty limited until I found my birth mother and got more involved in the Indian community here in Sacramento.

It's interesting that even though a white family raised you, you have strongly embraced your culture, and it's so much of who you are and what you do.

Absolutely. You can't take that away from anybody, no matter what. I think most of us do find our way home, or at least attempt to, and it was very important and continues to be a very important part of my life.

Say more about that. What does it mean for you to play the Native American flute and to be so ingrained in your culture?

There's a sense of pride and a sense of destiny or purpose. Now I see the big picture. I can see like an eagle from up high, and away from the situation. I look down now and I see that this was all a part of the creative destiny for me and the plan for my life. It was destiny that I played that classical flute and moved into the Native flute, and did something very different, which is play this instrument as a woman.

Your audience may not know that it's not traditional in our culture, if you are Plains Indian or Southwest Indian, for women to play the flute. Now, I have to clarify that because there are over 550 nations, and we all have very different rules concerning the Native American flute, that some of us didn't even have flutes in our nations and tribes. It really depended on where you were from. If you were Plains Indian or Southwest Indian, only men used this instrument, and it was used in courting.

Did you know that when you first picked it up?

I did not know that. I had not listened to a lot of flute music at
that point, and when I bought my first flute, I didn't rush out and
go get flute music. I really wanted to retain my own style, whatever
that was. I didn't know where I was headed with it, so I just enjoyed
it and played it. I loved it! I loved the sound. I loved creating
melodies with the instrument. So, no, I did not know it was not a
traditional instrument to play.

**What drew you to play your first Native American flute,
and how did it differ from playing the classical flute?**

It was so much more freeing. I didn't really come to it with
the attitude that you've got to play bars of music, and everything
should be a traditional, a European style of making music. I had a
friend who had a store in old Sacramento and he carried a couple
of flutes. Because I play the flute and I had been collecting world
flutes at that time in my life, I thought I needed to have a Native
American flute. The first time I picked it up and played it, I got
people in his store applauding. I thought, wow, this was easy to
play. But then, I did bring my skills from the classical flute to the
Native American flute, so I could put my fingers over the holes
and figure out how to play it. That comes pretty easily to me
anyway. I love almost any kind of instrument and can figure out
how to make some noise out of it, at least. That was my first
introduction to the Native flute and it just felt like:
Aaaaaahhh...this must be meant to be.

It just felt right for you.

It did, it really did.

51

Tell us about buying your first flute.

It was $150, and I couldn't afford it. I was working part-time at the Gallery of the American West, which is a Native American gallery. I couldn't afford this instrument, so my friend let me put it on layaway *and* take it home. Usually you put something on layaway and you get it when you finish paying it off. But this was a friend and he let me take it home, and I started practicing right away. That first flute took a couple of months to pay off, and was actually purchased on layaway.

A good purchase, I would say. So when you started playing the flute, it felt natural to you, and then later on you found that it wasn't acceptable for a woman to play this instrument.

Right, depending on the tribe, what tribe you were from. Certainly, people let me know that.

How did you deal with that?

Well, again I became more determined to play it well. Saying no to me was not the right thing to say because I became more adamant about it. I thought, you know what? I love this instrument. I'm going to play it. It feels so natural and I enjoy it, and forget what everyone else says. The creator gave me a gift and I'm going to use it, and that's what we're supposed to do when we're given a gift. Those were my thoughts.

There's a definite pattern there, that when people say no to you, you become more determined.

Yeah, and I'm not really a stubborn person. That's what's interesting. But I was determined.

You knew what you wanted.

Yes, yes.

There was a point in your life when you actually hit bottom. When would you say that was?

Probably around the time I found my birth mother. I was a single mom and on welfare, and being in the welfare system is quite devastating. I hadn't ever been in that place before where you have to stand in line for food stamps, and it's just devastating, and it became a vicious cycle. It was difficult to get off welfare, but I slowly was able to do that. Then I remarried, and that helped as well, but those were some really tough years, being in the system and being very poor and uneducated. I had big dreams for trying to get out of it. I dreamed my way out.

Say more about that. What helped you get out of that rut?

I did a lot of writing. I did a lot of journaling, even back then. I have volumes and volumes of journals. I would write about my dreams. Then I started writing some short stories, and one I wrote was about a young welfare mother. It was my story, basically, and how she was discovered having great talent and was able to get herself up and out of welfare. And again, I visualized it.

In addition to visualizing and writing, what action steps did you take that helped you move from that bottom place to the high place that you have attained in your life today?

I was always creative. I kept in touch with that creative side of myself. I started painting again and doing sculpture. Friends would acknowledge me and say, "Wow, you're talented. Maybe you should be doing something with this talent."

That was really key: having people in my world–my family, my circle–encourage me and see that I had talent and nurture that.

I did more painting, and then I ended up taking some of my sculptures into the gallery where I ended up working. A girlfriend of mine talked me into taking my sculptures down to that gallery. She said, "You're going to take that stuff down there and show him." She really pushed me and really encouraged me to the point of saying, "I'm coming to pick you up at 9:00. Have those sculptures boxed and ready; we're taking them in." And thank you, Terry. We have a 20-year friendship. She is still a dear friend, and we have been able to encourage each other back and forth in our attempts to want to be creative and be artists. So, I did have a lot of encouragement from people who believed in me.

I can hear how much of a difference that made.

Yes, and it was wonderful. I look forward to being able to do that for someone I see who's coming up. It's all about mentoring. I think that's really important for us to do as Native people, as artists, as women–support each other and get each other moving when we're in a slump, and I certainly was supported that way. She had seen those lonely, hard, difficult years and was just such a dear sister and friend.

Have you had other mentors along the way?

I have. I attempt to find mother figures. I have a dear friend I call Mother Sister Friend. She's been a very important person in my life as a young mother coming up, and having struggles that we have, as women. I can always call and rely on her. She's got more wisdom and more years than I have and similar experiences. She's able to coach me and encourage me through those times because she's been in those situations too. I really think that having a mentor in my life, having a Mother Sister Friend, and being able to seek that out–knowing that that's something unique, maybe even lacking in your life, that kind of relationship–is important. I found mothers. I've always had an elder in my life.

What about mentors or teachers in the music field? Have you had many role models or mentors who were musicians?

My father bought me one of Buffy Saint Marie's records in the 70's and he said, "Hey, Mary, look this is another Native American woman who's into music and singing." I was introduced to her in the late 60's, early 70's by my father, understanding that I was seeking these little snippets of Native American culture. It was very thoughtful of him to point out this wonderful woman whom I discovered in the 70's and continue to enjoy. I've worked with Buffy Saint Marie, and that was really a pleasure, because she was one of the only Native women that was out there at the time doing anything. So yeah, Buffy, go!

And, of course, Rita Coolidge, being part Cherokee, although a lot of us didn't know that until the late 70's. But I think Buffy Saint Marie was huge for me in my life, as were a lot of folk artists. Joan Baez is another. I liked that these women were women of color who were strong, who were making statements. I know that I remember Joan Baez stepping forward and playing her anti-war music during the Vietnam War and I liked that. These were wonderful role models for me.

To summarize, you've had lots of role models and you found your instrument; you had some natural ability and you had

lessons along the way, but what has it really taken for you to be successful in your field?

Passion. I tend to be a passionate person about everything, whether it's taking a drive along the countryside and loving the fact that I'm away from the city, or passionate about a sunset, or passionate about a specific Brahms piece, passionate about my children, or passionate about a lover, passionate about music. I tend to be passionate all the way around, the full gamut. I'm very excited about life; I enjoy it, almost every aspect of it. The negative has good things to offer, so I think that that's part of my nature, and it needs to be expressed. I've always had so much energy that I needed to get that out. I found the way to do that in performance and playing.

There are a lot of people who are good and really enjoy making music, but don't take it to the level of success that you have.

I think I was in the right place at the right time. I had an innate knowing about how to do that, about how to put myself in the right place at the right time.

I found out that Joanne Shenandoah was going to be doing a PowWow cruise. I thought, what an interesting concept. I had just discovered PowWows myself in the Sacramento area. I had been attending PowWows for the last 10, 15 years, and I thought it was interesting and I liked her work, and I always felt as if I was going to work with her someday. It was like a knowing that I was going to work with her, or maybe a desire that I wanted to work with her.

I made it happen. I held a moonlight concert on a full moon to raise the money to go to the PowWow. We waited until 9:00, when the moon was up over the building, and I had tiki torches all around.

It wasn't very expensive to put on. We did it at a Unity church that liked me and my music, and they offered to let me use the grounds. I think we charged $10 a ticket, and I raised enough money to be able to put myself on that cruise.

I called the cruise director and said, "I'm booked, I'm coming on this PowWow cruise to Mexico, and I play the Native American flute, and I know that Joanne Shenandoah is going to be playing, and I would love to work with her and meet her. I'm offering my services. I'd be willing to open for her. Do you think this would work?" So, I sent in a demo tape to him, and I guess he ran it by her and she said, "Cool, yeah, yes, let's do it." That started a whole series of things that happened in my life.

I want to stop just right there to reiterate what I heard because I think it's important. You saw an opportunity that felt right for you, and that you really wanted to do and didn't have the money to do it. So you found a way to make the money to do it.

Yes.

Without even knowing if you'd be able to open for her.

Right.

Then, you contacted them and you took the steps without having to know how it was going to turn out. You just got committed to it.

Yes, that's right, because I figured if I go on the cruise, I'll be meeting her anyway, and I would still have taken a flute if the cruise director had said no.

You would have gone either way.

Oh yes, I was already planning on going. Besides, I needed a vacation.

It served many purposes.

Yes, yes, but I visualized it. Again, I pictured it. I pictured playing with her and opening, I could just see it.

You pictured it, you visualized it, and then you took inspired action that was in alignment with that picture.

Yes, yes, and somehow I just made it happen. Again, it was determination, the drive. The drive was very, very strong. I don't know where you get that from. I think that's innate. I think you are born with it or not. I think there are many people who don't realize that we have that power—that it *is* there for everybody. I think that a lot of us just don't tap into it.

I put myself in a situation where it ended up being very advantageous, as Joanne and I just fell madly in love with each other. We're dear sister-friends to this day. I truly consider her a dear friend as well as a wonderful, accomplished artist in her own right. It really was the start of a wonderful friendship. It blossomed into her saying, "Hey, you should check out my record label. I will send them a copy of your demo; I think they will love you." And, of course, Silver Wave Records said, "Another flute player? I don't think so." Joanne said, "But this is a woman." They didn't really understand the correlation, the importance of that at the time. Then I was offered a couple other deals by other record labels, and Silver Wave thought, um, OK. And that's when I went with Silver Wave Records.

All from a PowWow cruise.

Would you tell people what a PowWow cruise is?

Well, a PowWow, of course, is a Plains Indian event where we gather and dance. It's competition dancing. The cruise was the concept of a gentleman named Dave Underwood who thought it would be fun to have a PowWow onboard a ship, and have it be a themed cruise. The concept was very interesting and it continues to go on today.

It sounds like it brings together Native Americans in one place to dance and enjoy time together.

Right, that's right, and concert music.

You've had quite a few goals in your life and you tend to be really determined and visualize them and take steps to achieve them. I imagine with the classical flute, you practiced a lot. Is practice just as important with the Native American flute?

It *is* important. I teach my students scales. That's really huge. It was huge when I was 10, and nothing's changed. You've got to get adept on your instrument and learn it well. The only way to do that is to do your scales and fingering exercises. Some of those basics are still really important in how I teach the instrument. But there's a lot of freedom in this instrument as well. I like that it doesn't have parameters and boundaries–those bars and measures and counting. Although, as a recording artist, certainly I have to be somewhat accountable for rhythm, and take that into consideration.

There's so much freedom surrounding this instrument, and because it's in a pentatonic scale, which is a particular scale, almost any of the notes that you play together are right and sound good. It's very encouraging for people who've never played a musical instrument to pick up the Native American flute and play it relatively quickly and easily. It's very conducive to all kinds of folks to play it. It's just an incredible instrument. It has a draw.

There's something about the Native American flute. One of my flute makers believes that it affects our alpha state, that it affects our brain waves. I have students who say that they'll play and their dog just looks at them funny and just kind of sits there, aaah. I certainly have experienced going into a room of 500 children when I'm doing an assembly, and once you start playing the flute, everyone mellows out. Teachers will play my album when the kids come back from recess, and it's calming. So there is something about the Native American flute that draws us.

I like the freedom that it gives *me* as a musician, as an artist. Even though I love the classical flute, there are definitely parameters, rules, and regulations–everything's within a certain parameter. With this flute, you have total freedom.

Is teaching something you also love to do?

I swore I'd never be a teacher because both of my parents were educators; I never wanted to do that. But I find myself teaching and really enjoying it and being a natural at teaching. Maybe it comes from those years that I would go in and help my mother with her art class, or music class, and really assisted my mother with the kids and working with them. I have students for flute and I also teach workshops throughout the country and teach embellishment of the Native American flute. Wow, I ended up being a teacher, oh my God.

You've now been supporting yourself fully on your music for four years. In what ways do you support yourself through your music?

I teach, I do workshops, I do concerts. I love to go to universities and usually, I do a lecture that's tied in with a concert that night. I talk with music students or Native American study students or women's studies, and I travel throughout the world. I've done film scores and worked on people's projects. I've done a lot of compilations, which of course, does generate royalties. The concerts are my major source of income. Of course, the CD's, but you don't really make money from CD's. CD's are the tool to get my name out there so that I can do the live performances, which is the bread and butter of this business for me.

It sounds as if you travel a lot.

I love it, yes I do, I do.

As you speak, I hear that you love everything you do.

It's that passionate kind of thing, yeah, I really do. I'm made for this business, and you really have to be. I hear traveling salesmen say, "Oh, the road, oh, never again, I've lived out of suitcases."

But when you're doing something you love, it makes a huge difference, and I think that's really important that we do what we love and find a way to make money from it. It started very small for me. It didn't happen overnight. It's taken 30 years. I read books as well. I went out and found books on how to do certain things at the beginning of my career so that I could learn how to be a good businesswoman.

That's important, isn't it?

It really is, yes.

How do you balance the life of a musician with family and other obligations?

That can be a challenge. I think my children help ground me. I think my children are a balance for me because it keeps things real when I still have to do crisis management from a cell phone 2,900 miles away sometimes. Of course, when I'm here, there are the mommy things you do, and so I think for me, that's been very grounding and very balancing.

And I pray. I'm not a religious person. I was raised with mainstream religion. I really follow more of a Native path, which includes smudging and prayer and sweat lodges. There's a place I go to out here where I sweat and have friends who do the same, and so I seek out like-minded people, people who are on the same spiritual path or journey. That really keeps me balanced because you have people you can talk to about these things in the spiritual realm. I think all those things really help to keep me balanced.

How old are your children now?

11, 14, 19 and 21.

That's a lot to balance.

It is.

And do you think it's working for them, too?

Oh, they're just so proud. We went to a restaurant the other day and someone came up and said, "Everyone in the back's trying to figure out if you're the music lady or not. Are you the woman that's been on TV?" The local media here has just been incredible. So my children are enjoying the spill-off of that. And of course, the kids' friends say, "Wow, is your mom the one that won the Grammy? Wow."

Ben, my oldest son, is talking about taking some music business courses in college. He's seen me struggle with management situations, and, he's saying, "I want to help my mom in her business." I don't know whether he will or not, but it's on his mind and in his heart to want to try to help or be a part of it somehow. I think my children caught the bug a little bit, and of course, there are musical instruments all over this place. I buy keyboards for them and guitars; they're certainly surrounded with music.

What advice would you give someone who is considering either a musical career, or following any passion that they might have?

Follow your heart. Follow that knowing, that innate knowing, and sometimes you don't know. My daughter says, "But I don't know what it is I'm supposed to do." Being aware that when that comes, you *will* know. It's okay as a young person to be searching these things; that's why she's going to college. You might not find what your passion is until you experience a little bit of the world. For her to take Yoga classes, and music and history and art, she's going to find a little bit about what she likes. That's why I think higher education is important for our children.

How old were you when you discovered the Native American flute?

I was 30-something.

So it can happen anywhere along the line.

Anywhere, anytime.

What's next for Mary? What dreams do you have that still need to be fulfilled? What can we expect to see in two years?

Oh, lots. Someone said, "What are you going to do now that you've won the Grammy?" But this isn't the end at all; that was just one of my goals.

I see myself going into the world music vein. I mean I have loved world music forever. I was collecting flutes from all over the world before I was playing flutes from all over the world, or Native American flute. I'm very drawn to cultural things. I'd love to work with someone who plays Sitar, like Anoushka Shankar, or Tabla Players, East Indian flutists, or diggery do from Australia, and Hawaiian music. I really see myself playing with other players in the world music vein, at world music festivals, and maybe getting a reputation as being a good player for these kinds of venues and artists.

Even as you were talking about it, I heard you say, "I see myself doing this." You've got it visualized.

I do! That's true, very true.

So, we know it's going to happen, we will expect to see these things.

One of my fantasies is to work with YoYo Ma. I think that the cello and the flute are glorious together and there are other artists, of course, I'd love to work with. Envisioning that, yeah, is certainly important.

I'd like to travel and do my music, and see places in the world that I've only heard of. I'm fascinated by that. I thoroughly enjoyed being in a different country. I haven't been to Peru a lot, but it's probably one of my favorite places. There are so many Native people down there, too, in Peru. So I've got big plans. There are so many things I want to do.

It is clear that even though you wanted the Grammy and you visualized it, you didn't see it as being the end-all-be-all.

No, no.

It's important to note because nothing is, is it? There's always more that we want, there's more to aspire to or else what challenge would there be in life?

That's right. I want to put my children through college, that's another goal. There's a lot of things going on and so much to look forward to. I'm really, really excited about how the Grammy will be a tool for me, another tool to be able to achieve my goals and what I want to do, which is make music. So it's not just the end all, it's a tool, and wow, what a tool.

This is great because it's going to help me do those things I really want to do.

Mary, I want to thank you so much for sharing your story with us. I think there's a lot of value here for people, and we just really appreciate you.

Well, thank you, thank you so much.

Three Key Success Principles Plus Coaching Questions and Action Steps
• •

Mary Youngblood

Key Success Principle #1:

Visualize Every Step of Your Dream and Watch the Magic Unfold

The muscle movement that helps us physically take action in our lives begins in the mind. This is why all great golfers, tennis players, basketball players, etc., visualize themselves making a shot beforehand. An experiment conducted by Alan Richardson, an Australian psychologist, found 23% performance improvement among subjects who visualized every day for 20 days. In his paper published in *Research Quarterly*[1], Richardson wrote that the most effective visualization occurs when the visualizer feels and sees what he is doing.

In addition, when you see and feel yourself accomplishing something, you are producing positive emotion. When you feel good, you are not only more inspired to take action, but you also naturally attract more things to you in alignment with how you are feeling. You become a magnet.

I was talking to an associate one day who was complaining about debt. I asked her to visualize her credit card balance at zero and to notice how good that would feel. She did that and the next

---

[1] Sports Visualizations by Keith Randolph, www.llewellynencyclopedia.com/article/244

week she was ecstatic; a relative had offered to lend her the money to pay off all her debt. Her credit card balance was actually going to be zero, just as she had imagined it. She had attracted to her someone who would help her attain the goal she visualized.

If you are not able to visualize yourself accomplishing your dream, you may be blocked. Typically, blocks are nothing more than our gremlins[2] whispering words of doubt, such as "Who do you think you are?" or "No way." If this is the case, you might want to try visualizing yourself accomplishing one small step toward your dream rather than achieving the whole thing. As you perform these small steps, your confidence will rise and your gremlins will get quieter.

How Mary Visualizes:

Mary visualizes regularly with amazing results. As a young girl she dreamed of being the crème de la crème at anything and everything from the World Series to the Miss America Pageant. Even as a child she could see herself walking up the stairs and onto the stage. Mary always dreamed of being the best at something and she visualized herself doing just that. When she learned about the PowWow cruise, she knew she wanted and needed to be on that cruise and to connect with the lead performer. She visualized it happening and took action in alignment with her vision. Down the road, that connection helped her get a record contract.

Coaching Questions:

1) What is your dream?

---

[2] Gremlins is a term borrowed from *Taming Your Gremlins* by Rick Carson

2) Are you able to visualize yourself attaining that dream?

3) When was the last time you visualized yourself doing something? What happened?

Call to Action:

1) Take a moment right now to visualize yourself having accomplished your dream. Conjure up as much detail as you can.

If you can see it, you can make it come true. Don't worry if it is blurry. Just see and feel it happening to the degree to which you are able. If you can't see the whole thing, visualize yourself taking one small step toward the dream. Feel the excitement of having achieved your goal. It is important that you combine both the picture with the positive emotion of actually having made it come true. Hold that vision for 68 seconds. When you hold it for that long, you start to bring it to you. Do this every day.

2) Prepare visually before taking the next step. For example, if you have a meeting with someone to gain his or her support, visualize yourself having a successful meeting. See yourself being calm and confident and the other person responding positively. Now, when you go to the meeting, your brain will automatically seek to live into the image you created in your mind.

Key Success Principle #2:

Defeat the Ambiguity Monster: Write to Focus

The longer you can focus on seeing yourself accomplishing your dream, the better. If you can't hold your visualization for at least 68 seconds, try scripting it out. Scripting is like visualizing except when you script you actually write your dream out as if it has already happened. The idea is to write with as much detail as possible and as much enthusiasm as you can muster. Scripting can be even more powerful than visualizing because when you are writing, your mind is forced to focus on what you are writing.

Both scripting and visualizing not only feel good and send positive images to your mind and body, they often result in inspired action. (See Key Success Principle #3.)

Journaling is another form of writing that can be a catalyst for your dreams. Often our thoughts get tangled in our mind and it is difficult to get clarity. Journaling is a way to get your thoughts out of your mind and onto paper. It is the act of writing your thoughts in a notebook. There are many different forms of journaling. One way to journal is to do a mind dump. When you do a mind dump, you write and write and write to empty the millions of thoughts from your brain so you can then begin to think clearly.

Journaling can also be used to shift your thoughts. To do this, first write about what has happened and any concerns you have. Next, ask yourself questions to forward your thinking such as, *"How can I go forward from here?"* Allow the pen to write down whatever responses come to mind. You could also type your responses on a computer. Use whatever method works best for you.

Where Mary Wrote:

Mary scripted when she was at her lowest point in life. At that time she wrote a short story about a woman who worked her way up and out of welfare. She saw herself being discovered as having great talent and becoming successful as a musician. Interestingly, that's exactly what happened. Mary didn't call this scripting nor did she know how powerful an exercise writing that short story was. But it is no coincidence that her story became reality. Mary also journaled frequently.

Coaching Questions:

1) What do you want to change in your life?

2) How frequently do you journal about this?

3) If you resist doing this, is there something you don't want to see?

Call to Action:

1) If you have journaled in the past and stopped, this is a great time to start again. If you have never journaled before, there is no time like the present. Commit to journaling your thoughts 2-3 times per week. Use the journal as a way to express your thoughts as well as a tool to ask yourself questions that will move you forward, such as *"What could I do differently?"*

2) Respond to coaching question #1, "What do you want to change in your life?" On a separate piece of paper, write a script of you already having made that change. Make it vivid and exciting and better than any story you could possibly imagine. When you read it, it should bring a smile to your face. If it doesn't, keep embellishing it until it does.

3) After scripting, notice what action, if any, you are inspired to take. Go ahead and act on it!

Key Success Principle #3:

Easy Does It: Inspired Action Always Trumps Forced Action

Inspired action is joyful action that is in alignment with your dream. It is action you want to take and the idea of it brings a smile to your face. The inspiration behind it often comes as a result of an "ah ha!" moment or it can be self-generated from scripting (see Key Success Principle #2). When you take inspired action, you are aligned with what you are doing and things flow naturally.

Contrast this to action that you are forcing yourself to take regardless of whether you feel like doing it. Maybe you are in a bad mood or have a headache but decide you have to take this action and keep trudging forward. The likelihood is that if you take action from this place it will take you twice as long to accomplish your task or goal or there will be obstacles that come up along the way. It's like swimming against strong currents. This is because there is a part of you that is resistant to it; for example, a voice inside says, 'I want to rest or take a break' or 'I just don't want to do it.' In this case, you have a choice: keep pushing ahead or take a break and come back to it when you are refreshed.

Where Mary Took Inspired Action:

Mary listened to her inner knowing and acted in alignment with it. After writing the short story about a woman getting up and out of welfare, she began creating paintings and sculptures again. These pieces were sold in an art gallery and she started bringing in money.

Later Mary sensed that she needed to buy a Native American flute. She took inspired action, went to the store, picked one up and played it. In that moment, she automatically knew this was right for her. The rest is history.

Coaching Questions:

1) How often do you force yourself to do something even when you are resistant to it?

2) How productive are you in these moments?

3) When was the last time you took action that felt inspired? What was the result?

Call to Action:

1) Begin listening to yourself more. Notice when something feels good and when it doesn't, when you want to do something and when you would rather be doing something else.

2) If you don't want to do something, ask yourself what would feel better? Choose to do what feels better and give yourself full permission to do it.

3) Even if you have a deadline to meet, give yourself permission to take breaks as needed and then come back to your work. Notice whether you are more or less productive with this method.

4) Observe your inspired thoughts and "ah ha!" moments and act on them.

My Key Learnings from This Chapter:

1)

2)

3)

Chapter #3:
Loral Langemeier

Financial Coach and Entrepreneur

*Single Mom Becomes Millionaire
and Teaches Others To Do The Same*

Chapter 3

Loral Langemeier
Financial Literacy Coach, Speaker and Millionaire

"We aim above the mark to hit the mark."
- Ralph Waldo Emerson

I'm here today with Loral Langemeier who is a financial coach, speaker, entrepreneur, self-made millionaire, and a single mom.

We all want to know how you got where you are, so, let's back up a few years. My understanding is that you built your first business while you were still in college, is that right?

Yes. I had an aerobic and personal training business while I was in school. I took that on to grow it into a larger, corporate, wellness-consulting business in the Midwest. I would consult with corporations on everything from back injury prevention to stress management and nutrition. My work centered around employee productivity and the employees' behaviors, and our intention was to have them show up at work in a more productive and healthy way.

I did that for quite a few years until I went to the Gulf of Mexico. I was in a contract with Chevron, and I flew around in helicopters and visited offshore oilrigs. I did that same sort of work with employee productivity and the health of the employees for several years. I was based out of New Orleans.

Let's stop right there for a moment. What made you decide to start your own business while you were in college?

Freedom. The All-American Dream. A lot of people say the All-American Dream is having your own home; I think it is having your own business. I grew up with both parents who never were employed with anyone. My father farmed and ranched, and my mom was a caterer. So I knew the lifestyle and knew what it took, but I didn't know what it took financially. I knew energetically what it required. Also, I've been an athlete all my life. Doing work in this area, health and wellness, was great. When I got into corporate America I noticed that we were working diligently to get people healthy and yet sending them to a sick culture. So then my next career was a lot of organizational development and employee training on leadership communication, values, and alignment. I kept saying, I was getting people healthy and sending them to a sick culture. That's when I switched gears.

Talk to us about the role of mentors in your life.

I've had mentors forever, since I can remember. Even through college, a president of a bank was mentoring me. Coaches were mentoring me. A lot of people think of mentors as the big stage names and the authors, but there are so many mentors that are just in people's back yards. My current company, Live Out Loud, pertains to that: It's how to be in the conversation about money to get what you want, and understand how this game's played, because there's a lot of unspoken rules to the game.

You started out with both your first mentor and your first business in college.

Absolutely. And in any subsequent move I made, I would first ask myself, "Who's doing it the best?" "Who's successful?" "Who's doing this the way that I'd want to do it?" Then I would go and seek them out. For instance, Dr. Ken Cooper was a prominent figure in the health industry–and he's still very well known—so during college I went and interned in Dallas with Ken Cooper. It was phenomenal.

You sought out the best from the get-go.

Absolutely. In my late 20's, I switched to an organizational corporate training company. Again, I sought out who was doing it really well, who knew how to get inside corporations. I went and worked for them for a while–not as an employee, but I offered my services and my time. They said, "Well, you don't have enough skills," and I said, "I'll fly anywhere for free if you let me learn from you."

What I notice about a lot of people is that they're unwilling to stretch to that place because they say, "I don't have time," "I don't have this," and "I don't have the money to fly." I would move things around to get what I needed. I would get to where I was headed a lot faster by learning in the field versus going back to a traditional school and thinking there was going to be a traditional model. There are entrepreneurial models, and you can adopt one of those, and still get to do it your own way. That's what I love about it.

You sought out these people and were willing to volunteer and work with them for free in return for their teaching you.

Absolutely. I have people learning from me all the time, too. They'll just want to be in the office or be at an event with us. Events are usually where people get an enormous amount of experience. They get to see what I call 'the game.' They get to see how any game–whatever game (or business) you choose to play– gets done. You can read all you want, and I'm a huge proponent of reading, but where the real learning happens is where I call "out on the streets." You need to see, experientially, how the game gets played. You get to see the business from the inside out.

I bet you shortened your learning curve considerably doing that kind of research.

Well, that's why I am where I am, in my fourth business. In six months we grew this business to a million dollars, and it's because of the pace of that accelerated learning. I believe that everyone who's going to take on an entrepreneurial business and really have a millionaire mindset must get very efficient about the road map. You need to know how to take what I call the shortcuts, not from a quality standpoint, but shortcuts.

I'll give you an example. People I work with in coaching are new entrepreneurs who want to learn QuickBooks themselves. I don't want entrepreneurs doing their own books; I want them to hire a bookkeeper. So instead of going to a bookkeeping class, we offer them a shortcut. "Find somebody who's really good, who has a bookkeeping service, hire that person for a day and get specific knowledge on your business. Set your books up right away. Cut it down to one day. Don't sit in the general class and then try to figure out how to apply it. Get specifically what you need, and just shorten the learning curve." That's just a simple example, and that can get expanded in all sorts of areas.

You tell entrepreneurs to do what they're good at, not spend their time on tasks that aren't their greatest strength or what they love doing.

Well, this pertains to all business administration work. Especially really new entrepreneurs and new investors spend a lot of time planning to plan and planning to get organized. In my opinion, their main activity needs to be revenue producing. I always call it the fastest path to cash, and they need to be driving it, and getting incredible support around them.

I get the sense you have a lot of energy.

Enormous energy, and a lot of that is because I love what I do. It was really interesting because I knew even back with the company that I was running for corporate development that it wasn't quite what I wanted. Then in 1997, I met Robert Kiyosaki, and Sage International, and John Burley; I just met a whole culture of people who were really doing the 'how to get rich' thing. *Rich Dad, Poor Dad* was just coming out. I became the only facilitator/ trainer of the Cash Flow Game and master distributor. Again, I started another whole company. But it was based on wealth building, and financial literacy.

After being with the Cash Flow organization for five years, we made a transition on our own. And a lot of that is because I'm ready—it's my time. I've been mentored by a lot of people and now it's my time to turn the tables. I've developed my own work in wealth building. When I say wealth building, I mean how do you build three prongs of business into your life: in trading, in real estate, and as an entrepreneur. I know a ton of people who I call straddlers: they're in one job and they really have their foot and their heart somewhere else. And they want out.

They have a lot of road maps to help them do that. Mentoring is a huge piece of it. Clarity about yourself is a huge piece of it. I have always been living on purpose around freedom because I know that's just a huge value of mine. When I found this work, I felt at home. I would do this work for the rest of my life. I know that what I'm here to do is teach financial literacy because it comes so naturally. So, to return to the question of energy, it's natural— I'm doing what I love to do.

You weren't always doing financial literacy. You were doing other things. But it sounds as if you always picked things that were a good fit for your skills and your interests, is that right?

Yes, and I would do them in a way that I knew the learning could come forward into any niche. I knew I was building a skill set by working with large corporate America. I would see from an operational standpoint what it took to build a large organization. When I was being mentored, I would watch how the small organizations worked efficiently and how they outsourced. I would always be watching. These were building blocks that got me here. And I didn't know that it wasn't "it" then. I didn't know when I was in the health industry that that wasn't the place that I'd end up. I know wealth building will continue to be it, but I wouldn't be surprised if I ended up owning a mortgage company and taking the company public. I mean, I have lots of interests. I have a real estate company, as well.

You're diversified.

Yes. I want to speak to that, too, because I think one of the biggest entrepreneurial mistakes is when people diversify too fast. For instance, a lot of people who come to us for coaching have four or five things on their plate, but none of them are in revenue. When I say revenue, I mean, I want a minimum of $100,000 gross business when I'm working with somebody. Minimum. I would rather see that be more like a half million, and then they take on another business. Unless they have a big team.

I think people misconstrue what multiple streams of income are. They have four things going, they have four interests, but none of them are really businesses. In our entrepreneurial program, the first chapter is to look at whether you are building a business or a hobby. What we see is a lot of multiple hobby doers who would love to have a business, but they don't know the structures and they need to be seeking mentors who really know how to build business. Those would be two important first steps.

You see people trying to spread themselves too thin between different things and not getting off the ground with any of them?

Correct.

So the idea is being focused on one, get it really solid and successful before you move on to the next.

Yes, and solid and successful is in the numbers. Get it to revenue, the fastest path to cash. Get it to revenue, do the tweaks, work the systems, so it can continue to flow when you go away a little bit. The next tactical move I see people making that I think is a mistake is they move away too quickly to the next thing they want to do.

They are driving that current revenue; it's their energy, it's their vision, it's their passion. Even if they have good people around them, if they make that move too quickly, I see their businesses struggle. A lot of people will come to us for coaching or mentoring and their first goal is to replace themselves. They'll say, "I want to replace myself in three months." And I'll say, "You mean a year, possibly two years." They're stunned. "No, I need it to be done now."

It takes a while. For 12 years now, in addition to mentors, I've hired very specialized coaches who are playing a way bigger game than I'm playing, in a niched area. For example, I have a marketing coach, I have a Web coach; I have very specific coaches. Right now I'm working with four different coaches. I have somebody who does business valuations that are highly sophisticated.

So the other thing that I notice is that as you get into this, a lot of people don't want to spend the money on specialized knowledge. If people have never read *Think and Grow Rich*, finding your burning desire, having a plan, and having that plan in specialized knowledge is critical. It's similar to what I did most of my life, which is that I find very specialized people who are playing a bigger game and are the best at it, and I hire them.

I notice the words you use to describe this. You say, "invest" in a specialized coach. It's another investment in you.

Absolutely, it's good tuition.

How did those investments pay off? My guess is that you more than make back what you pay on those investments.

Absolutely. A lot of people will look at our coaching program and say, "I just can't afford it," and I say, "How can you not afford it?" Because if it's not us, who else? Somebody has got to help you, because what you're doing isn't working. You're stumbling around looking at *Business Plans for Dummies* and trying to figure out how to build a business.

You're trying to figure it out all by yourself.

And trying to figure it out versus using a successful model to emulate. It doesn't have to be exact, but it needs to be close. I always say that any of your own personal learning is tuition; whether it's an asset or a liability, depends on you.

When I sit down with my coach in marketing, we set up a ratio. For example if I'm going to pay $5,000 for a program, I want back $20,000, just to break even. I want back a rate of return and it's not the coach's job in that situation to make that happen. It's their job to guide me, but it's my job to put all the wheels in motion to get that kind of revenue back.

So, you can monetize most of your tuition programs. Even from reading a book. How many people buy a $15 book and say, "Wow, those were really good ideas," and then do nothing about it. I mean, you see that all the time. I think it's up to you as to whether your investment is an asset or liability.

Loral, when did you make your first million?

When I was 34. It happened when I was pregnant with my son. I'm a single mom and nothing got me more motivated than knowing that I would be coming into that lifestyle of being a single mom. And it pertained to the way I wanted to raise Logan. I have very specific ways that I wanted him raised–I wanted a creative learning environment for him. What that would require was a greatly increased revenue stream.

I got highly motivated and really started at that point. I got very efficient about raising OPM, which stands for other people's money. Again, I found someone who's been a phenomenal business partner and investing partner. He's older and had a lot of experience in real estate. I went to him and I said, "Let's do this together. You have the experience, I need your credibility, and I know a lot of people with money." But they weren't going to invest with me alone because I hadn't done as much real estate as he had. He and I partnered and got an enormous amount of investor money. We bought huge amounts of real estate. It happened very quickly.

You found someone not only to mentor but also to partner with you.

I do a lot of joint ventures and have a lot of partners. There are times where I'm the senior to other people. It's about finding the right matches in your business model to get what you want.

Another program that we launched in 2003 is called WealthDiva.com. At that time we were really focusing on women and wealth and what we found is that women's and men's orientation to money are extremely different. Women play more to not lose versus playing to win. Men are more aggressive.

Women are more cautious and are likely to think, "I need to make sure that it's secure and I won't get hurt." Men will joint venture faster because women will have more trust issues about the relationship. I always say that trust is not so much about an innate trust, but that women, more than men, do not know how to do the deals, they may not have enough confidence to do the deal, so they don't tend to get into the deals. That causes their business development to be a lot slower.

Where do they get the knowledge?

You go back to mentors, the coaches. The other part of it, too, is learning the industry that you want to be in. This again pertains to having specialized areas. A lot of people are doing so many different things–for instance, they might have a network marketing business and a catering business, and then on the side they want to do speaking and coaching–so they have all these things going on. Let's just say you have four things going on. If you work a 12-hour day, that's only three hours of effort towards each initiative. That's a huge distraction to cash and then they'll go into credit card debt; they end up in a cycle and then they end up just going to get a job because this entrepreneurial thing is too hard.

Say something about good debt versus bad debt.

That's huge. Debt is incredible. A lot of people say that debt's one of the biggest expenditures, although taxes are actually worse. People don't know anything about taxes, but we'll get to that one in a minute. Debt is one of the single most crippling things for most of the entrepreneurs and investors that we see because they didn't manage their debt well, which means it's affected their credit.

What's the difference between good and bad debt? To us, bad debt is a lifestyle debt, it's consumer debt. It's your Macy's credit card, your Sears credit card, and all of the things that you couldn't afford and so you overspent. An example of good debt would be if you own a real estate property that's worth $100,000 and you put down $20,000, so $20,000 would be the asset side, $80,000 would be the liability side. That's good debt. We would never want you to pay off the $80,000.

Say more about why.

If you have $100,000, why would you put it all into one asset? In fact, we usually do 90/10 so we only put 10% down because we can use the 10% to go buy a second property. Instead of having one at 80/20, we would rather have two, one at 90/10, and the second one at 90/10, both producing cash. We would rather leverage.

We have a lot of multi-millionaire clients who come to us for basically two things: foundational work–to clean up their foundation around their entities, their tax, their insurance, their trusts and to accelerate into non-traditional investing. A lot of them have enormous equity in properties. I don't know how many people have $500,000, $600,000, $800,000 in one property where they could leverage that to buy more. And we're not talking about over-leveraging; we're doing this very strategically and smart, but it's giving you ideas that there's so much available.

A lot of people say, "How do you get into real estate?" I say, "Well, do you even have a realtor?" "No, I've never talked to one." So, find realtors, lenders, appraisers, and real-estate investment clubs. Same with trading: go to trading clubs. There's tons of learning involved, but go ahead and get immersed in it, because what's also interesting for people to realize is that in every niche business, there's what I call the subculture. These are the people who really know how to get it done, and those are the people you need to find. If you read, The Millionaire Next Door, most of them live below their means at some level. They're not flashing their wealth. They still have a great lifestyle and they know how to make money. But then there are the people who are flashing their money who have, in essence, what I call, a leased life.

It's the same phenomenon in business. In a lot of the dot.com failures, those companies hired a lot of hotshots who didn't know how to run a business. That was one of the factors that led to their collapse. There are multiple factors. And then there's the real deal subculture that do make it happen. They move the concepts into tactics. If you can't do that, you can't see how your plan is going to make cash, then it's still in hobby land.

Backing up for one minute, what I think I heard you say is bad debt is lifestyle debt, and good debt is debt that produces revenue.

Right. Good debt would be debt that is either attached to an investment or an asset, or something that's producing cash. You get to a point where you have to have some money rules. Some people ask, "How long do you hold on to a property that's not producing cash?" Strategically, I'd look at a lot of ways to get it to produce cash before I just offloaded it. I wouldn't throw it into bad debt just because it's not producing cash. It also could be appreciating. There are a lot of variables around that. But essentially, good debt is attached to an asset that is producing cash, and bad debt is just sitting in liability.

You just touched on how millionaires live versus people who are flashing it about and in debt. How would you describe the millionaire mindset, what does that mean to you?

My first word is capacity, and the second one would be leadership. I'll start with the leadership.

From a leadership perspective, it's leading your life the way you want to, not at the expense of others. A lot of people consider rich people to be bad and I don't believe that. Most of the people I know who are really wealthy give back enormous amounts. We have a program where I'm a CFO of a non-profit life school and we give back a percent of what we make to them and encourage our people to do it as well. So, I say lead your life the way you want it, lead your business–there's the leadership of your teams.

Capacity is a function of leadership. How large can you see the big picture? The frame for a millionaire mindset is knowing you'll have it and that you're attracting it all the time. When I look at building a business, it doesn't occur to me to think outside of a million dollar status of a business. Because, then why would I do it? I've already done it before; I know how to build it.

Yes, but did you always think that way?

I always thought big and tactically. Probably the biggest challenge with a lot of mentors is teaching an understanding of the how to's. A lot of people are wandering around looking for how to actually do things.

I'll go back to the example I used earlier. In my experience, I would go into corporations to see how they did their training. Many in what I call my 'old network' would say, "I can't believe you're going to get on the airplane and they're not paying you." Too many people are not being willing to rearrange their schedules for some really enhanced learning. They're not willing to spend the money on a coach, not willing to do what it takes from a capacity standpoint; they use excuses in their life to stay small.

What I'm hearing is, be willing to do whatever it takes.

You have to. A new mentor of mine said something brilliant the other day. She said, "In the beginning you have to really stretch that capacity." We were talking about doing what it takes and I said, "How in your own words do you explain that to somebody?" We know intuitively how to do it, but to explain it to somebody is more difficult. I watch my coaching clients transition to the other side and say, "My gosh, I get it now."

It's interesting because how and when the transition happens in a person is elusive. You will look back and say, "I cannot believe I was thinking that small." You start to see how deals come together. You start to see how the world really works. You start to see how money can get made with a lot more ease.

In my experience, part of leadership and capacity is learning to lead others. You let go of your bookkeeping and you hire a bookkeeper. You hire a personal assistant. You start increasing your capacity. Yes, it costs more money to do that. So the millionaire mindset is about expanding it, not about fitting all your bills in this tiny little box because this is all the money you make. There's money *everywhere* to be made.

It's also living in that place of possibility, remembering that there's a lot out there, that I'm not limited.

Yes. My mentor's words were, "You have to go way out of balance to get back into balance." Because it's almost as if we'd have to take some of these entrepreneurs and stretch them so far to such a level of discomfort and then let them come back, but in doing that, we've stretched our capacity.

Say more about getting them way out of balance and then bringing them back. What do you mean by that?

Many of my beginning entrepreneurs have a set lifestyle. For example, they like to get up at a certain time, they have kind of a methodical routine, and they're unwilling to give it their all. There are times–for example, in our transition of being on our own last year–where the amount of hours our entire team had to put in, and the amount of energy we exerted to focus on the restructure to get "Live Out Loud" up and running was enormous. I mean, enormous.

We had to spend money for extra staff, and we had to ensure that our staff was totally committed. On a new launch like that, new entrepreneurs are likely to say, well, I can't afford more. Then, make it bigger and give more away! We give people performance bonuses for helping grow the company.

Going way out of balance means you need 100% of your focus on one thing in order to grow it. If you coach them that way, new entrepreneurs will do it.

You'll hear a lot of people such as Zig Ziglar and Bob Proctor, say that there's a price for success. I would always say, there are *conditions* for success. And one condition is that you have to really want it. What precedes that is people will say, "That's a good idea." I hear people say that all the time. But unless you know that you really, really want something, you'll hit a roadblock and then will back off and say, "Well, I was busy anyway."

There isn't a day that I would be too busy to keep living my vision. It's that clear–that this is what I'm up to on the planet. This is what I'm here to do.

And you're really passionate about it.

Oh yeah. And it isn't even about me anymore. It's really about giving back, and being a vehicle of information and experience for other people.

When did it switch from being about you to being about other people and what you're providing for them?

Well, that's a great question. It wasn't when I hit my first million, because it still felt like a chase. I know a lot of people know what that means: you're still chasing it. Probably last year, when my capacity was way out of balance, it became my business and my work to be about others.

You've arrived, so to speak.

I know that the work we're doing is pure; that is, it's pure attention to support and help others, and there's calmness there.

You know the best visual I've seen to describe that is in the movie, "Catch Me If You Can." The main character, played by Leonardo DiCaprio, is running down the runway and Tom Hanks is following him and he says, "If you look behind you, no one's chasing you." That's what I see with entrepreneurs; I often use that metaphor on stage now because what I see with entrepreneurs is that they're chasing the 'it's not enough,' which is really a psychological issue. They're chasing and chasing and chasing. Kiyosaki called it running on the treadmill or racing around the rat race. When you know that you don't have to race anymore is when the shift happens. There's a calm that's present, a peace. You just know: it's going to happen. In fact, what happens then for a lot of our wealthy clients who are already there, when you get to that place of calm, the money comes. The cash comes back so quickly and it requires managing that. A lot of people say when it comes, it comes fast. It does come fast.

Would you say that is because you are more in a place of peace or a place of allowing?

A place of allowing, a place of receiving, and also a place of clarity, because money won't come to you if you are confused. I'm really clear about that.

Money doesn't come to a confused bank account. Why would the universe deliver it there if there weren't a plan for it–and a plan to make more? Really knowing, having clear plans is essential.

Some of the first homework I would give to anyone who's reading this is to get really clear. I would say down to the penny. A lot of people would say, "I make about $5,000 a month." Well, is that $4,250, or is that $4,970? You have to get really clear about where they are: regarding income, expenses, assets, liability. And that means clear about the truth. No exaggerations. Where are you in debt?

We always say our program's a little intimidating because their first homework is full disclosure.

Bob Proctor's one of my phenomenal mentors. He's been the mentor I've had the longest. He said, "Give me your checkbook and your calendar, and I can tell you what's been important to you."

We want to look at the patterns of what's been important, and what got the person to the current state of affairs. From there, we can recreate three things: Psychologically, we need to re-look at what's going on. Foundationally, we need to look at the daily behaviors that are continuing to create the problem or the success, whichever it is. And then, how do we accelerate it for them? Because everybody may want the American Dream, but it's important to clarify what that means to him or her, and what their version of that is.

So, Loral, people would say you are a risk taker...

I wouldn't say that, though.

I know. How do you balance or calculate your risk, or prepare for what you're going to do, so that you know it's a good risk?

Education. Learning, knowledge. Out of that comes confidence. When I'm confident, it doesn't feel like risk. I would associate risk with being more tolerant of other people. When you invest in a PPM, a private place memorandum, or an IPO, a start-up company, you're really putting your money in the stock market. If you invest in Intel, for example, you're investing in the brains of the people, and those brains also have emotions. To me, the bigger level of risk is other people's emotions and other people's drama and how that will affect the performance of my assets. When I look at risk, it's more about who I am involved with, and that goes back to leadership. How do I interview people? How do I choose partners? How can I be in that relationship? But I reduce that view down from an enormous amount of knowledge, which increases my confidence and which increases my clarity to make the decisions about where I'm going.

The other thing around risk is that a lot of people are abdicating their responsibility to their wealth building. They say, "Well, Susie knows better," or "John knows better," or "My uncle's friend's friend; he's been in the market for a while, he knows how to invest." What you're doing is putting your money out there with someone who may or may not have your best interests in mind and will not necessarily have a clear strategy. You don't have to *know* it all, but you have to *lead* it all. You don't have to know about the details of trading in the market, you don't have to know about the details of real estate, but if you're going to be in it, you need to know enough to lead them and say to them, "This is the kind of rate of return I expect and, by the way, I want a monthly phone call so we stay connected."

It's keeping more control of your money and your investments versus putting it way out of your mind. One of the furthest out from your own responsibility and involvement that you can put it in is 401K's. I'm not a basher of 401K's; I think 401K's are fine, but they should not be the only assets to offer people. Too many people have their whole life wrapped up in one 401K. That's a very dangerous model, especially given today's economy, and there's ways to diversify that out, allocate that out, so they'll be in a more solid position.

That's exactly the next question I was going to ask you. How do you deal with the ups and downs of the market? My guess from what you're saying is, by not having all of it in there so it's not all at risk.

Absolutely. If you give it all away to other people to handle, and it's too far out from you, that is, you abdicate it to others, get back into it so you can position yourself. You've got to be able to make moves, because it's a very dynamic game. I think the other thing that's amiss in the wealth-building world is thinking that you're going to make a financial plan and then you don't ever have to make a decision again.

I'm making decisions daily, weekly, monthly, although not the big, big canvas ones. What we want people to do is get clear about what they want when it's Financial Freedom Day. When people can have the life they want, what's the amount of cash that signals that day is here? Then we can back into the plan. The clearer you are out there, at 10 years, 20 years, 30 years from now, the clearer and more direct your short-term decisions will be.

Most people are just wandering around from day to day making decisions, not knowing where they want to go. That means they're wandering and they'll make a particular move, and then something will happen, so they'll make another move.

When you're really clear about where you want to go, short-term decision-making gets easy and emotions come out of the money decision, which is really why Wealth Diva is going to be such a huge program for women. Stop making emotional decisions about money and start making financial decisions based on numbers. It's not difficult to read them; you just have to practice, just like in any other sport.

I always use my health and wealth metaphors. I think everybody has money muscles, they're just atrophied little guys. Get on a conditioning program. The first time you look at a P&L,

you're going to say, "What is this? I don't know how to read it. I don't even know what the variables are. I don't know what a chart of accounts is." Of course you wouldn't, because you never looked at it before. You also never knew how to ski down a black diamond ski slope the first time you got up there; you start on the bunny slope and then you go up to the green slope, and then you go to the blue slope, and then you helicopter.

What would be the first thing you would suggest to people who want to become more knowledgeable about investing in the stock market? What's one step they can take to improve their abilities and their knowledge to feel confident in their decisions?

Get a coach, get a mentor. I say that somewhat in jest because clearly that's what we do. We help people do that. But there are people everywhere who do that. There are investment clubs that you can join. And start reading. What I notice about a lot of people is there's only a certain contingent that really wants to know how to trade like a day trader. You'd have to know about the indicators, the variables, and how a market really works. Not to the extent that a person with an MBA would, but start getting educated.

Real estate investment clubs are probably one of the best ways to learn if you want to be interactive. What I find is that if you just read a trading book, you still have your own limiting thoughts and your own limiting capacity wrapped around your decision-making. In situations where you're interacting with others, you'll see and hear new perspectives. Go to chamber meetings. There's so much networking going on. Be in the conversation about investing.

One big problem, however, is that people go to listen and they don't ask questions. If you're not getting an appropriate answer, you're not asking the right questions. What we teach in our leaderships programs is that your job is to be an incredible, powerful questioner. Ask, ask, ask, ask, ask.

Is it that people are afraid to ask? They're afraid they'll look stupid?

Right. Traditional educational programs generally are in essence, saying, "Stacey, if you had read your homework assignment, you wouldn't have to ask all these questions." And parents say, "I know best." I would like to eliminate that line from the entire American population of parenting, because they don't know best. I think it's brilliant that the child's asking a question, and yet, what they're doing is making the child wrong for asking. We have to recondition all those muscles so adults will get back into the conversation. Learning is the first step, and starting to get clear about a strategy.

I'll have people call me after a teleseminar and ask, "Should I cash out of this stock and go into treasury bills, or should I cash out of this and go into gold, or should I do this and then go into real estate?" And I would say, "It depends. It depends on a couple of things. Number one, where do you want to go, what's that bigger vision? And number two, where are you now, based on everything else?"

This is actually a million-dollar tip because if you go to a financial strategist or a planner or CPA and they give you advice without looking at your whole picture, they have a clear agenda about getting either paid on an insurance policy, for instance, or they're getting paid on an annuity. They're getting paid on a net financial instrument and they're not caring about your whole strategy.

Your job is to lead them and say, "This is my strategy." If they say, "Well, no, we just need you to buy this," walk on. Go interview other people. Go get somebody else who's going to be with you in the growth of your whole plan. The community of these kinds of strategists that partner with you is small. A lot of people say, well, a CPA doesn't know. There's a lot of brilliant CPA's, but you have to interview for more of a strategic one, not just one that files tax returns.

Does that make sense?

Totally.

Isn't this fun? Love this.

Here's a question for you. You're very successful and you're growing and you're expanding, you obviously love what you do. You also have a young child. How do you balance this big success with raising this young child?

We have an enormous amount of quality time. I believe that it does take a small village to raise a child, so I have a private nanny and her family. I live across the country far from my family, my biological family. But I have a whole new one. I have an enormous community that's been around me and supporting me in raising my son. We have a "two-sleep" rule. We never sleep apart more than two days. He has become a little traveler; he's traveled to lots of continents. He's been well educated, and he has a lot of play.

My #1 thing, above my business, is balancing my life with my son. It's a high priority. The little Chairman of the Board even comes on stage often. I include this subject, balancing professional and personal, in the work I do because I know part of my mission is to model, especially for single women, that this game can be played. It can be played in a multi-million dollar status and you don't have to go on welfare; you don't have to play small about it.

You don't have to be ashamed about it, and you don't have to be a victim about it. So there's a huge message in WealthDiva.com about all sorts of women, but specifically, I know there wasn't a mistake that a single mom is showing them that there are different ways to succeed at this. And you have to be willing to ask for the support. I have enormous support around me, so I do get to have it all.

It's delightful to hear you say that, because most people would assume that because you are so busy, your child takes a back seat, but I don't hear that at all.

No. We're going to leave on an airplane this afternoon. We're going to the Midwest, so my parents are going to come down and stay in the hotel and take him to the zoo and take him to play while I do my thing on stage. We'll spend our evenings together. A lot of people say, "When you get home, you have to do all these domestic tasks." But I don't, because I hire assistants. This would probably offend some people, but this is the way I've designed it. When I get home, I have meals made, somebody's already gone to the grocery store, and somebody is already helping with the laundry. Most families are included in all that. When I get home, I get solid time with my son for three to four hours every night. It's different because I've designed it differently. I've gotten support so that I get the freedom to live that way and I don't have to do all the errands when I get back from being on the road.

That's the biggest theme I've heard throughout this interview: how much you have gotten other people to help you. This is no one-woman show. You have a lot of people on your team, personally and professionally, from mentors, to assistants, to CPA's, to realtors, to nannies—all over the place.

All over the place. It's interesting because they get their vision, too. For instance, with my nanny. I refer to her that way, but she's a dear, best friend to me, and the woman who helps raise my son. She's doing her own absolute best work. She says, I'm here for children and I'm here specifically for yours and she's a phenomenal teacher, a phenomenal learner, and a phenomenal role model to my son. We're very aligned about how we want him raised, and so she is with him during the day.

My point is that other people get to live their visions through some other people's larger visions, but as long as everyone's aligned, and as long as everyone wins, it all works.

In a lot of these models, you'll see one person win at the expense of others. That's absolutely not how this model works. Everybody wins.

We need to bring this conversation to a close. Tell us what your Web sites are.

WealthDiva.com. LiveOutLoud.com. And another one that is my direct mentor program is LoralsBigTable.com.

I'd like to end with this Big Table story. You know how there are some large families and they have the big family gatherings around the big table and then there's the small table that all the children are relegated to. What I've noticed over time is that when I was pretty young, I went and sat at the big table. Nobody told me I had to go back. What I want to say is that in life, a lot of people are waiting for an invitation to the Big Table, and they're not giving themselves permission to just go sit there and design their life big. They're still sitting at a little table. I want to invite people to come design their own Big Table.

Great story. Thank you so much for sharing with us, Loral. I know that we could talk to you for hours and we'd love to just pick your brain, but you've shared a huge amount with us about how you've gotten here and your philosophies. I know that people are really going to get a lot of value from that.

Three Key Success Principles Plus Coaching Questions and Action Steps

• •

Loral Langemeier

Key Success Principle #1:

Shorten Your Learning Curve by Learning from the Best

You can learn from the people who are barely getting by, from those who are doing fairly well or from those at the top of the heap. That's what this book is about. Its purpose is to provide success principles and philosophies from those who have excelled. They've already been down the road and you can learn from their experience. Why reinvent the wheel when someone else already did a great job of inventing it?

Several years ago when I was thinking about writing a book, I knew that I wanted to learn how to market it from the authors of *Chicken Soup for the Soul.* After all, they had sold more books than anyone. At that time they were not offering a course on this subject but now they are and I recently attended Mark Victor Hansen's Mega Book Marketing event. From all of the ideas presented there, I can pick and choose what works best for my style and situation.

How Loral Learned From the Best:

Loral was willing to do whatever it takes to learn from the best. She would first ask herself, "Who's doing it the best?" "Who's successful?" "Who's doing this the way that I'd want to do it?" Then she would go and seek them out. For instance, Dr. Ken Cooper was a prominent figure in the health industry so during her college years she went to Dallas to serve as an intern with him.

In her late 20's she sought out who was doing organizational training really well, who knew how to get inside corporations. She went and worked for them for a while–not as an employee, but by offering her time and services. They said, "Well, you don't have enough skills," and she said, "I'll fly anywhere for free if you let me learn from you."

Later in her life she formed partnerships with people when they each had something to offer to complement each other. In doing these things, Loral accelerated her learning.

Coaching Questions:

1) Are you willing to do what it takes to accelerate your learning and make your dream come true?

2) Of all the stories in this book, notice which ones resonate with you the most. What can you learn from them?

Call to Action:

1) Name three people you could learn from. (Remember, these do not have to be big names; they could be your next-door neighbor, a coach, or a friend of a friend.)

2) If there is an investment involved in learning from this person, have the intent to monetize that investment; i.e., intend for a return on capital that would make it worthwhile.

3) Contact the person you most want to learn from at this time and see what is possible. Do it *today*.

4) This book is full of success tips from some of the best. Learn from them. Write down a key learning that really calls to you and a corollary action step from every chapter in this book. Also write down a date by which you will accomplish it.

Key Success Principle #2

Laser in on One Idea, Business, or Income Stream at a Time

One of the challenges Loral talked about is people diversifying too quickly. This is true whether you are trying to build multiple streams of income or are just working on several different ideas at one time. The key is getting the first stream or idea up and running, producing good revenue, and having systems in place so it will keep running without you before going on to the next unrelated stream. Remember what Loral says, "Several things going on at one time is a distraction to cash."

As a person with many ideas, I know this can be challenging. At one time I was beginning to invest in real estate, writing this book, and maintaining my coaching business. I was making progress, but it was slow progress. When I put the real estate to the side, the momentum for this book increased. The stress factor declined substantially and the joy factor increased accordingly.

How Loral Focused on One Stream at a Time:

Loral has many ventures but she didn't create them all at the same time. She learned to get each business up and running solidly and have a team in place to maintain it before going on to the next one.

Coaching Questions:

1) How many streams or ideas are you working on at once?

2) How much progress are you making on each of them?

Call to Action:

1) Pick one idea and focus on it solidly for a period of time. Notice any difference in your progress.

Key Success Principle #3

Make All Your Debt, Good Debt

The great majority of Americans have large amounts of bad debt. Bad debt is lifestyle debt or things that you buy that you really can't afford at the moment. Estimates of the average amount of credit card debt at this time range anywhere from $2,200 to $10,000 per person. This does not include debt that people assume to buy high-end expensive cars, trucks and boats that they cannot afford. Our society encourages this. You can lease a car with hardly any money down but never own it, and if you own a business you can write the lease off on your taxes. You can buy a boat and finance it for as long as 15 years with some lenders. All you have to show for this debt is a lifestyle: a lifestyle that you have to work really hard to maintain so you can pay off all that debt. Many people feel trapped in the "rat race." Maybe it is your lifestyle that is keeping you trapped.

I was taught that all debt is bad debt. But this is not true either. Good debt is income-producing debt or debt that is attached to an asset that produces cash. Examples of good debt are real estate investments, business investments, and capital expenditures that increase your bottom line.

How Loral Maximizes the Use of Good Debt:

Loral does lots of joint ventures with other people. When first beginning to invest in real estate, she did a joint venture with a top real estate investor where she brought in other people's money as her contribution to the partnership. Of course she had to pay these people back, but she was able to do so out of the proceeds earned from the real estate investments. She could not have invested at the level she did had she not used other people's money. And by bringing other people's money to the table, she was able to learn from a top real estate investor. Loral continues to use other people's money to purchase real estate today and has established a separate business to do so.

Coaching Questions:

1) How much of your debt is good debt and how much is bad debt?

2) Are you willing to forgo a certain lifestyle and start living below your means while building your dream?

Call to Action:

1) The first step is to start paying off your bad debt. Start by paying whatever you can afford towards your credit card debt every month. Start somewhere even if it is only $10.

2) The next step is to start a short-term savings plan so that you have reserves and don't have to get into bad debt when emergencies occur. Make a commitment today to put some amount of money into savings every month, even if it is just $5.

3) Once you have paid off your credit card debt (typically the highest interest), pay off your car. By paying extra on your car payment and applying it to the principal every month, you will pay it off early. Then keep your car and drive it as long as you can. Put the money you would have used to make that car payment into savings or an investment every month so that you will have saved enough to pay cash for your next car or use that money to pay off your mortgage. Soon you will be totally lifestyle-debt free.

4) The next step is to start educating yourself on income-producing opportunities using other people's money. This is good debt. Do it now. You don't have to wait until you have paid off your bad debt to get started.

My Key Learnings from This Chapter:

1)

2)

3)

Chapter #4:

Tom Glavine

Professional Baseball Player: Atlanta Braves and N.Y. Mets

Voted Most Valuable Player in the World Series Despite the Odds Against Becoming a Professional Athlete

Chapter 4
• • • • • • • • • • •

Tom Glavine
Professional Baseball Player,
N.Y. Mets and Atlanta Braves

"What I am actually saying is that we need to be willing to let our intuition guide us, and then be willing to follow that guidance directly and fearlessly."

- Shakti Gawain

I'm here today with Tom Glavine, who is a professional baseball player, formerly with the Atlanta Braves, and currently with the New York Mets. Tom is a two-time recipient of the Heissman Trophy and the Cy Young Award. He was voted MVP of the 1995 World Series. He is married with four children.

How long have you have been playing professional baseball?

About 20 years now; 3 years in the Minor Leagues and 17 years in the Major Leagues.

Hard to believe?

Yes, very hard.

Do you remember when you first picked up a baseball?

When I was a young kid, four or five years old. I was just playing around and took a liking to it. I started playing organized Little League ball when I was seven, and played each level along the way from there.

When did you start dreaming about playing baseball professionally?

Probably in junior high school. By then, I think you're at the point where you start seeing, or at least understanding things that you like and things that you're interested in. I certainly was interested in sports and in professional athletes enough to know that it was something that I would love to do someday. I probably didn't seriously think I would have an opportunity to do it, though.

But you knew you wanted to.

Yeah, I knew I wanted to. I knew it was a dream. I thought it would be great, I just didn't know if I'd realistically ever get an opportunity to do that, but fortunately, I did.

Lots of kids dream of being professional athletes. The difference is that you turned it from a dream into reality. What do you think made it different for you, in addition to the fact that you obviously have athletic ability?

I think athletic ability is obviously a big part of it. There are plenty of people who dream of being a professional athlete but, realistically, don't have the athletic ability to do it. I've also seen other guys who have the athletic ability to do it and never achieved it, so it's a combination of having the ability and having the desire.

Becoming a top-notch athlete is not without sacrifice; you have to put in a lot of work. When I was an amateur athlete, whether it was Little League or in high school, there were a lot of vacations that I didn't go on and a lot of things I didn't do because I had a game or a practice.

You have to be serious and willing enough to forego that stuff, and participate in what you're supposed to be participating in. I would say I'm going to practice today, and some guys would say I'd rather go to the beach with my friends, or I'd rather go do this or that, and the desire wasn't always what it should be.

It sounds as if they weren't really committed.

Some of them weren't, no. There are some guys I've seen that had a ton of talent but got distracted by things that took away from their ability to really buckle down and be serious in their work habits and their preparation.

So you had natural ability, but then you also practiced a lot.

I had natural ability, but there are plenty of people in the world who have athletic ability. There has to be something that separates the guys who make it to the next level and the guys who don't. I don't know that my talent at that age was any better than anybody else's. I'm sure there were a lot of guys that had more talent than I did, but I've been able to get to this level and become successful at this level. I think a lot of that has to do with my commitment and dedication, and willingness to work hard at it.

It has been said that you have a "never-give-in" attitude. What does that mean?

Well, I know what I need to do during the course of a game to be successful and I really don't deviate much from that. I think there are times where you may not be pitching as well as you would like to, for instance, or the score is a certain score and you try not to make mistakes.

In my case, I've always had the ability to trust myself to know what it was that I would need to do and then try and do that. I would stay stubborn about it. I take the approach that I know this is what I need to do and I'm going to try and do it. The result may not be what I want it to be, but I know that what I'm trying to do is the right thing and it's just a matter of executing it.

It sounds as if that attitude is what got you into the Major Leagues to start with, and it's also what has helped you prevail and win awards.

I think so. The guys who I've seen become successful have a dedication and a commitment that is different from the guys who don't make it. You have that commitment throughout, whether it's in a game or in a practice or off-season. You know what you need to do to be ready and you're committed to doing that.

How do you handle the difficulties or the failures when you don't pitch that great game? How do you handle those setbacks?

You just take the approach that you can't be afraid to fail. You know you're going to fail. You know it's going to happen. I don't care how good a year you might have as a pitcher, you're still going to lose some games. No matter how good your team is, chances are that your team's going to lose at least 60 games a year. So, you're going to have downtimes.

To me, the key to being able to be successful is learning how to deal with those bad times, taking something out of each one and putting it behind you as quickly as you can and getting ready for the next one. Especially in baseball, you don't have time to waste thinking about it; you're playing every night. As a starting pitcher, you have a little bit more time and that's what makes our jobs a little bit harder. When you have a bad game, you can't go out the next night and do something about it like most players can. You've got to wait five days. So the key is to have that bad game, look at it, learn from it, figure out what you did wrong, what you can do better, and then use that mentally to build for your next game. You try and do those things better and improve upon them.

There's not a lot of time to sulk.

No, there's not. Even for a starting pitcher, even though you're not playing the next night, your team generally is, and you still need to be in a good mood and be committed and do what you can to try and keep a good attitude on the bench. If guys see you moping around and sulking, they're going to know it and it just kind of gives them a bad feeling.

Do you set yourself up as an example for other people to follow?

I try to, particularly for younger pitchers. You have to show them that win or lose; you're still coming to the ballpark the next day with the same commitment, the same desires. There's nothing worse than a guy who is always in a good mood and happy to be around when he has a good game, and then when he has a bad game, you can't talk to him and he's mad at the world. I mean, players can't stand guys like that. They want you to be the same person, win or lose.

Granted. if you have a game where you don't perform particularly well, you're going to have a period of time where everybody kind of respects your space and gives you some time to cool off or get over it, so to speak. But relatively quickly, you're expected to be back in the fold and be the same person that you always are. I think when you see guys who are like that–who are the same guy, in good or bad times–people tend to respect you for that.

Did someone teach you to be that way growing up or is it just something you picked up by yourself?

I think it was the combination of both of those things. I remember when I was younger, and particularly when I was playing hockey, my parents would try to talk to me after a game, and if I didn't have a good game or we didn't play well, and I was difficult to talk to, that was a problem for them. I remember my parents telling me, "Look, if we're going to take you to these events and you're going to play these games, then you're going to go into that locker room with a smile on your face, and you're going to come out of that locker room with a smile on your face. If you're not, if you're going to make it miserable for us, we're not taking you." So that kind of started it early on.

Then, as you go through the professional ranks and you pitch a little bit more and you get more experience, as with anything else, you learn how to deal with things a little bit better and a little bit differently, so it kind of grows on you over time.

What kind of encouragement or discouragement did you receive when you were growing up, for being a professional baseball player?

I don't know if there was any discouragement. It was more like facing the question of how realistic a goal that was. For example, I never approached it from the standpoint of wanting to be a professional athlete and that was all I was ever going to do. I mean, it was in the back of my mind; I hoped I got an opportunity, but along the way, I did everything else that I needed to do to be prepared for the very much higher chance that I would not achieve that goal. I did well enough in school to be able to go to college and be able to do other things. Then I got the opportunity to be able to play professionally and I took it and it worked out.

I always had my eye on being prepared for everything else first, and if sports came along and sports became a reality, then great, I would deal with that then. But I was more in tune with the real world, so to speak. Along the way I don't think I ever really got discouraged, but I was more encouraged to be prepared for that not to happen because, let's face it, the reality is that the odds of somebody becoming a professional athlete are pretty slim. You have to be prepared for the other stuff, and if sports comes along, then great.

You went for it but you were detached and you also had back up.

Yeah, I didn't put all my eggs in one basket. The things that should be taken care of were being taken care of and the extracurricular stuff sporting wise, I did that too. I did as well as I could and I just happened to get myself in a position where I had an opportunity to try it, and it worked out.

When you say you got yourself in a position, how did you do that?

Well, by performing on the field, performing on the hockey rink. I got myself in that position based on being a good enough athlete that somebody drafted me and gave me a chance to play. Then I was faced with the decision of whether to go to school and get a college degree or to take a chance on playing baseball or hockey. Inevitably, I chose to take advantage of my opportunity to play baseball, and it worked out.

You had been playing for the Braves and living in Atlanta and now you are playing for the New York Mets. Does that mean an actual move for you and your family, or are you commuting back and forth?

There is some commuting going on. I am there for the most part during the baseball season. During the off-season, Atlanta is still home and it's going to remain my family's home, so I'll be here. But during the six months of the baseball season, my kids will be coming back and forth on weekends during the school year and then during the summertime, coming up for little bit bigger chunks of time when they're not in school.

So, it's an adjustment. It's going to be a little bit of traveling for my wife, but I think it's an opportunity for us to see something different from a professional standpoint. It's an opportunity for our kids to see a bigger city—one of the biggest and most exciting in the world. It's more opportunity, and I think that they're excited about it. They're excited about going up and seeing a new city, and particularly New York, with all that it has going on and the history that it has. I don't know that they necessarily understand all the logistics that are going to go into the plans for making everything work, but they'll learn.

I can hear the challenge that it must be to balance family life.

It is; it's hard. Our family comes first; that's first and foremost. But even having said that, as much as we try to do that, there are obviously times where that becomes difficult and challenging. That's the most important thing to us, though, and that's part two of the growing up process of learning how to deal with failure. When you're a parent and you come home after a bad game, well, you know what? Your kids don't care. They don't care that you had a bad game. Dad's home and they want to jump around and have fun and play. You don't have time to sulk over whether or not you had a bad game. I mean, family is where it's at, and you try and juggle baseball around that and, at the same time, try and keep life for them as normal as you possibly can.

What I really get in listening to you is that family is a priority for you.

It is my biggest priority. Baseball was for a time, but once you get married and have kids, baseball falls back down the list a little bit. My family is certainly ahead of baseball. That's what matters. Baseball is a very important part of my life, and I'm dedicated to doing it as well as I can. But it's still about your family and doing right by them, and providing them with good examples and good leadership and trying to do that first, and being a good baseball player second.

I understand that you're also known as someone who is very charitable and likes to give your time and money to charities. Is that still the case? Have you been able to keep that up?

I find it's a double-edged sword. The more successful you are as a player, the better opportunity you have to be able to become involved in those things and raise money. The flip side of that is that with the fame and the family life, the busier you become, and the harder it is to do that stuff. But I do. I've got two events of my own that I do for charities to raise money, and certainly with guys on the team doing stuff, you're always saying, "Hey, can you do this event for me, and I'll do that event for you?"

So you're always going back and forth with each other, trying to help out. You become pretty involved, but it's fun. To me, it's still a humbling experience to be able to lend your name to something and simply because you're a baseball player, and people recognize your name, they're willing to support events or work for causes the way that they do. You're able to raise large amounts of money and know the difference that it makes for these people and for the organization. It's a great thing to be a part of.

What are your favorite charities?

I do most of my work for the Georgia Transplant Foundation and the Georgia Council on Child Abuse. Those are the two that I've done major events for over the last 10 years, so they're kind of mine. But there are so many good causes out there. That's part of what's hard: you try to figure out time-wise what you can and cannot do, and it's still always difficult for me to say, "No, I can't help you," or "No, I can't do that." You're not saying no because it's not a worthwhile cause, you just end up saying no to it because there's just not enough hours or days in the week to be able to go out and do all the things that people would like you to do, and take care of all of the things you need to take care of at home.

Right, you have to choose; whenever you say yes to something, it means saying no to something else. Any particular reasons for those charities?

No, particularly on the child abuse thing, no, absolutely not. My parents were wonderful and they were my greatest example in life, so I've tried to be the same kind of parent that they were for me and my brothers and sister.

I think more than anything else, with both of these charities, I just had a connection with the people who approached me about them. I enjoyed the initial conversation; I was intrigued by what they were trying to do. They caught my interest with their sincerity and their commitment to make a difference in the things that they were trying to do. More than anything else, I am drawn when I see a commitment from people to do what they want to do and the passion to do it. Those were the things that really grabbed my attention and made me say yes to those people.

Back to baseball, you've been doing it for 20 years now. How many more good years do you think you have left?

Realistically, three or four. I have a personal goal to try to win 300 games. So we'll see what happens. Physically speaking, unless something crazy happens, I think I can pitch four more years, no problem. I take good care of myself, and I haven't had any injury problems up to this point in my career, and I don't see why that would be any different. But it doesn't matter if you're 37 or you're 25; the chance to go out there and have a career-threatening injury at any point in time is still there. You just try and take care of yourself as well as you can. I'll try and give myself that opportunity to pitch the four years that I think I'm going to need, but there's just no way to prevent injuries from happening. I just hope that my health continues for the next four years the way that it has up to this point.

Do you have any idea what's next for you after baseball?

No, I don't. I've been approached, or at least talked to initially, about broadcasting, about coaching, and those are things that interest me. The only thing I'm certain of is when I'm done playing, I'm going to take some time off. I want to stay home and hang out with my kids, and hang out with my wife, and try and get myself to a point where my wife and I can look at each other and say, "You know what? It's time for you to get out of the house for a while." But I don't know how long that's going to take. The bad part about baseball is being away from home and the traveling. When I'm done playing, I don't want to do all that for a while. I don't know how long it will take me to get bored.

But you'd like to find out, right?

I want to find out, yeah. Initially, I just want to hang out and run around with the kids.

A lot of people make the mistake when they make a lot of money, of also spending all that money and not saving or keeping reserves for themselves. How are you doing with financial planning for yourself?

I've done extremely well. I think so much of that is your upbringing and the support people you have around you. My parents were lower-middle class. My dad was a construction worker, so the value of a dollar is still very fresh in my mind. And again, it's their example. You get what you need. You may not always get what you want, but you get what you need, and I've tried to maintain that. That's not to say you don't once in a while spend money that you never foresaw yourself spending as a kid, but it's all relative. I've tried to keep my eye on baseball as a short period of time. I have to live the rest of my life off the money I make, and you have to try and make smart decisions because of that and based on that.

I have a great agent and a great financial advisor. Believe me, when I pick up the phone and tell my financial advisor that I need a check, I feel bad about doing it. So they're obviously doing a good job for me.

It sounds as if you've done a good job of hiring the people who can help you in those areas.

I think the mistake that a lot of athletes make is that they hire people they think have their best interests at heart, but they don't; they have their own best interests at heart. I've been around my agent for a long, long time and he's a friend as much as he is my agent, and I know that he would never give me bad advice. The same is true for the girl who handles my finances. I've been with her for almost 13 years now. The first few years, you really don't make a lot of money. It's that initial period of time when they're helping you out, even though you're not making any money, but they're steering you in the direction of the decisions you're going to have to make and the preparations you should be thinking about. When you get to that point where you start making some money, it's not such an overwhelming thing for you. You know what to expect and what to do.

They've always known what my goals are. My goals have always been that when I'm done playing, I want to have enough money so I can maintain a certain lifestyle and not have to think about going back to work. If I want to, great, but I don't have to. Never assume that you have a bottomless pit. A lot of crazy things happen. You look at the last three, four years with the stock market and a lot of people have lost a lot of dreams in that period of time, but I guess I've always had my eye towards something bad like that happening, so I've been prepared for it.

There are a couple of themes that I hear in the way you approach life in general. One is that you're very goal-oriented, and the second is that you always seem to have a back-up plan; you prepare for the worst.

I think you always have to be prepared for the worst, and if it never happens, then great. But if it does, you can't be so taken aback by it that you don't know what the heck to do–you can't make rational decisions or you don't have your mind straight to even have a clue as to how to get out of it. It's important to prepare for that worst-case scenario, and if it never comes up, then great. All that you lost was a little bit of time in preparing. But if it does happen, then you're prepared to deal with it and make rational decisions. There are so many people who get into difficult situations, and then just don't make rational decisions, so they make their situations worse. I know that I make a lot of money right now on a yearly basis, but I'm also going to be retired when I'm 40 years old. I have an awful lot of life to live after that, so you need to be prepared for those years.

Is there anything else that you would like to tell people who are dreaming about becoming a professional athlete or have other goals for themselves? What advice would you offer them?

I think the biggest thing for people who have goals is: Don't lose sight of your goals, and don't get caught up in listening to people tell you what you can't do. Having goals is a great thing, but also, you have to be realistic about what your goals are. I think everybody wants to make a lot of money and be successful and rich and famous, and the likelihood of that happening for any one of us is not good. Having said all that, however, that doesn't mean you can't have those as your goal and you work your butt off to try and achieve your goals. In the meantime, make sure you take care of the basic things in life that you need to take care of so that you're prepared for whatever happens.

So many people try to bring other people down, and I think sometimes if they hear enough of that negativity–that they can't do something or the likelihood of their doing something isn't good– they start to believe it. I would just caution people not to get caught up in what other people are telling them they can't do. At the same time, be realistic about what it is you're trying to achieve and make sure that you have your back-up plan, or at least you have other ducks in a row so that if ultimately what you would love to do doesn't work out, hopefully you can land on your feet and do something that's pretty darn good anyway.

Sounds like really good advice.

Well, thank you.

Thank you so much for spending the time with us today. I know you've got a really hectic schedule.

Somewhat. But I appreciate the time, and hopefully, it will be good advice for people to hear.

Great, thanks so much, Tom.

Three Key Success Principles Plus Coaching Questions and Action Steps

• •

Tom Glavine

Key Success Principle #1:

Start with Talent: Season with Practice, Commitment and Persistence

If you are considering starting out in a new endeavor, comparing yourself to seasoned experts in your field can create a self-imposed roadblock that hampers you from seeing what you could potentially achieve. Many of my clients worry about whether they have enough talent to be really successful at something they haven't done professionally before. They fall into the comparison trap: comparing themselves as they are just getting started to others who have been building their expertise for 20 years or more.

Don't get me wrong; it is very important that your natural talents line up with your dreams. Otherwise, it will be a much longer, harder, and more frustrating path to climb. And who wants that?

However, even people with natural talent have to nurture and cultivate that talent. That may mean obtaining specialized training or gaining more experience. Usually it requires a combination of the two.

In addition to having natural ability in your chosen field, you must have other traits. Talent alone is not enough, nor is it always the most important thing. I always refer to Tiny Tim, the pop star of the 70's, as a great example of this. Some people loved his music, some thought he had no talent, yet people loved him for his uniqueness and he was wildly successful as a performer. William Hung, an American Idol castoff in 2004, is another example of this phenomenon.

To achieve your dreams, you must believe in yourself, believe in your product or service, have the persistence to do what it takes to succeed, and have the resilience to overcome the obstacles that come up. And sometimes, as in the case of Tiny Tim and William Hung, you need chutzpah (the guts to put yourself out there).

How Tom Enhanced His Natural Abilities:

Tom had natural athletic abilities and loved sports. He says there were a lot of guys just as good as he was who did not make it to the major leagues. The difference was that Tom made baseball a priority. He practiced frequently even when it meant giving up some other fun activities. He was committed to the sport and being good at it and he did what it took to get there.

Coaching Questions:

1) What are your natural talents and abilities?

2) How can you best use those abilities in alignment with your passions?

3) How could you enhance those abilities?

4) Do you believe in yourself?

5) Do others believe in you more than you do?

Call to Action:

1) If you don't totally believe in yourself, ask others who value your talent to describe how they see you. Then step into their vision of you.

For example, I have never seen myself as an artist. My husband thinks that I have talent in that area. I have decided to step into his vision of me as an artist. I bought paints and canvas and am learning some techniques and having fun with it along the way.

2) Commit to being the best you can be in your chosen field and create a plan to enhance your natural abilities over time (i.e., through classes, mentors and/or hands-on experience).

Key Success Principle #2

Handle The Basics (food, clothing, shelter), Then Reach for Fulfillment and Self-Actualization

In order to make your dreams come true, you need a strong foundation beneath you. Living your dream does not mean living in a fantasy world where you ignore your health, financial obligations, or loved ones. Actually, it's the exact opposite. If you are desperate and wondering where money will come from to pay for food or next month's rent, it will be very difficult to stay on track with your dreams.

People sometimes call me after they have quit their jobs or been fired and say, okay I'm ready to figure out what I want to do next and I need to do it in two weeks because I'm running out of cash. *Not!*

The best time to build your dreams is when you are financially stable or have some source of income to pay the bills, when your health is good, and you have a support team in place. If these things are not in place now, start building them. If you are out of work, find an interim job that pays the bills and leaves you the time and energy at the end of the day to work toward your dreams.

How Tom Takes Care of The Basics:

Tom makes it a practice to always have a back-up plan. That way he is not in a jam if one avenue or stream falls through. During high school, he practiced baseball continuously but he also kept up his studies in case baseball as a career did not work out. Later in life, he saved and invested his money rather than living an ostentatious lifestyle. Now if he has an accident or something happens to his career, he will still be able to pay his bills.

Coaching Questions:

1) If a major setback happened in your life or career, would you be able to take care of the basics?

2) How much money do you have in reserves? Could you live on this for at least six months?

3) Is there anything you could be doing now to enhance your ability to handle unexpected setbacks in the future? *Examples: purchase disability insurance, build your investment portfolio, create a second stream of income, or reduce lifestyle debt.*

Call to Action:

1) Decide how much money you would need to live for a period of six months to one year. If you have that much money now, make sure it is accessible. If not, start an automatic savings account and have an affordable amount deducted from your check each month.

2) Brainstorm ways to diversify your income and protect yourself so you are not dependent on any one source of income. Pick one method and implement it.

Key Success Principle #3

When Your Inner Voice Whispers to You, Listen and Then Act

Our higher voice is always talking to us. The key is listening to it and being able to discern between our higher knowing, our gremlins (negative chatter in our head), and our fears. To hear one's inner voice, it helps to get quiet, stop rushing around, and take a few deep breaths. Meditating or walks in nature can help you to get quiet. Once you are quiet, ask the question you want to know the answer to and be open to hearing it. The answer may show up immediately, as a "knowing" or it may show up as evidence in the real world.

When we follow our higher knowing or inner voice, we take actions that are in alignment with our true selves. And when we do what feels right for us, rather than what we think we should do or think other people want us to do, things flow better and we live a life that is in alignment with our highest dreams and aspirations.

How Tom Listens to His Inner Knowing:

Tom trusts himself to know what he needs to do and then he tries to do it. He acts on what he believes to be true. It doesn't always work out as he planned but he focuses on what is within his control. He knows that following his instincts and executing a plan in alignment with them is the best way to live.

Coaching Questions:

1) When have you heard your inner voice or an inner knowing the most clearly?

2) What was the experience like for you?

3) Did you do anything special to get in touch with your inner voice?

Call to Action:

1) Pick a question that you would like answered – something you feel uncertain about.

2) Ask the question to your higher self or write it down.

3) Let it go and be open to hearing or seeing the answer.

My Key Learnings from This Chapter:

1)

2)

3)

Chapter #5:

Stephen Pierce

**Entrepreneur and
Internet Marketing Specialist**

*Tenth-Grade Dropout Hits Bottom Before
Earning His First Million "Online"*

Chapter 5

· · · · · · · · · · ·

Stephen Pierce
Entrepreneur and Internet Marketing Specialist

"Your ability to get along well with others will determine your happiness and success as much as any other factor."
- Brian Tracy

I'm here today with Stephen Pierce. Stephen is an entrepreneur and an Internet marketing specialist.

You do a combination of things and they all are interrelated: Commodities and stock trading and consulting which you have marketed over the Internet and you've also made a business out of Internet marketing.

Yes, and all those activities basically happened by accident, Stacey. None of them was actually planned. One thing just led to another.

So you didn't have a plan for becoming an Internet marketing specialist?

No, not at all. I just wanted to be an entrepreneur. It actually started after I dropped out of high school; I only completed the 10th grade and I struggled along the way. A lot of people were more concerned about my future than I was because they were considering a model where you need to be educated so you can go get a good job. As far as I know, you can't even get into the military without a high school diploma now. So they thought: You're limiting yourself by not going to school and that was a big concern.

I used to hang on the streets, and then I ended up catching a stray bullet, and in March of 1995, I filed for Chapter 7 Bankruptcy. And things didn't get better. They got worse. And then I went back and tried to file Chapter 13 that same year, so that whole thing was kind of messy. I wasn't working a regular job because I always wanted to be an entrepreneur. So, in the process, I was trying different things, such as real estate, an arbitration business, vending machines, and I even had a badge-a-minute business—and all throughout the process, I was trying to become an entrepreneur. I was doing all these businesses with my whole heart, expecting them to succeed, but it just didn't work out that way.

So you experienced a lot of failures along the way.

A whole lot; I was basically "marinating in failure." And one thing that really devastated me along the way—it was so horrible—was when somebody really close to me and who meant a lot to me looked me straight in my face and said, "Everything you touch turns to dirt." I mean, that ripped the heart right out of me. I was left feeling really hollow. I thought, if this person thinks that of me and the only reference points I have are points of failure, what in the world am I going to do? And it was really lonely because outside of that, I didn't have anybody there saying, "You can do it, just keep on going." So I would get books and listen to different things that would come on Public Television, like when Les Brown would be on TV or Stephen Covey. I was reading books like, *Think and Grow Rich*—and my favorite book, by Mike Murdock, which is *Dream-Seeds*. I was reading them to get information that would support my thinking, which was: I'm not stupid, I know that what I want to achieve as an entrepreneur is possible. That's when I started to find points of encouragement. I found out that a lot of people who are successful today were outcasts, like the 'ugly duckling,' like the person who people would frown upon. Becoming an entrepreneur is an unorthodox road to travel. You don't do the "normal" things, you don't think the way "normal people" think, you don't look at things the way "normal" people do. It's lonely if you don't have other like-minded people to be with.

What kept you going? Was it that you were so committed to it? After one failure, many people stop. It sounds as if you kept picking yourself up and kept going.

I probably didn't know any better, actually. I still kept thinking, "Well, I'm going to do it." I was inspired and desperate. And I was really an independent thinker. What that one person had said to me crushed me because of the emotional bond we had—it was a family member—but I was soon finding I couldn't care less what anybody thought about me. I would even go to a pawnshop with things in order to go get something to eat. And I wasn't concerned about what people thought. Because I was still looking, I was still reading a lot of different books. I was looking toward the possibilities of where I could actually be if I kept pressing ahead. And I came to see that what I was experiencing was normal for an entrepreneurial life, even though a lot of people don't look at it as being normal. I just kept on going.

What do you think it was about being an entrepreneur that you were so committed to and wanted so badly?

The choices. You get to make so many more choices. I made an incredible discovery. A lot of people say, "I want to be an entrepreneur because of the financial independence." Well, I made a discovery about that which changed my life: Regardless of what you want to do, your financial independence is financially dependent on other people. It doesn't matter what you want to do and even if you take Rich Dad's Cash Flow Quadrant from the book *Rich Dad, Poor Dad*, and look at the way he divides it up: The self-employed, the employee, the investor and the business owner—every one of them has a certain dependency on other people. For instance, the employee depends on the employer, the self-employed person depends on clients, the business owner depends on customers, and the investor depends on brokers, floor traders, marketers and other corporations.

So trying to become financially independent by being independent of other people is the wrong way to do it. You have to build strong relationships, you have to build connections. You have to know that in order for you to succeed, you're going to need to have good, strong relationships. An album doesn't go gold or platinum without people buying it. People have to develop some kind of kindred spiritedness with people or something where you bond with people so they want to do business with you; they want to invest in your products or services. So the whole thing meant I needed to go out there, build relationships and just stay focused. And I also kept reading books on a number of topics. I recognized that anything was possible if I kept pressing onward.

Say more about the choices that you wanted from being an entrepreneur.

If you're bound to work for somebody else to pay your bills, you're going to have to be there at 9:00 in the morning or whenever your work hours begin. How much you make is going to determine what kind of different things you can experience in life, what kind of vacations you can take, what kind of car you can drive, what kind of fun you can have with your extracurricular activities such as entertainment, and how much money you can help other people with; that is, family members and friends. However, while there's still a dependency on other people, if you're running your own business, you can determine how much money you want to make by the type of relationships you build–the *quantity* of relationships, the *quality* of those relationships, and by being able to pretty much write your own check. Based on that, you can help more people. You can have more freedom to do whatever you want to do. You can work from home, or you can work from the beach, or you can buy that new car if you want. You get so many more different options. And if you see a friend or family member who needs money, it feels good to be able to give to another individual and help them out and be able to look at them and say, "Don't worry about paying it back. Don't be stressed by thinking you have another debt. Just take this and do what you want with it to help yourself out, and don't concern yourself with having to pay me back." So, there's a whole bunch more options you have when you have money. Life isn't always grand. It doesn't mean that you don't have your issues. But there are so many other things you can do when you have larger amounts of money.

Are you willing to share a bit about how much you've been able to earn? For instance, what has your income been, either annually or quarterly, from the Internet marketing that you've done?

Well, from the first time we collected our very first payment in the first quarter of the year 2000 up until now, we've made over $1,000,000 net cash selling Internet marketing products.

That's a little over a two-year period.

Right, a little over a two-year period. So far this year—it's now April—we've already made a net profit of over $140,000 from selling Internet marketing products. On average, we do $40,000 and $50,000 a month in net profits.

Not too shabby.

Not too shabby at all, working from home in my shorts! I turn around and play a few video games now and then to kind of break up different tasks, and then I watch the court shows on TV during the day. It's fine.

You also keep pretty busy in terms of your career.

Yes, our main thing is trade in the markets, using the commodities and stocks and stock options. So when the markets are open, the focus is on that unless the market is kind of quiet. Then I get to turn on the television. I usually just listen to the television as opposed to watching it, because there are five computer screens in here, and we're looking at different charts and formations to trade the markets. We have clients whom we advise, and we need to attend to their email and other communications. So it's a whole dynamic that goes on throughout the day. But the entire process is a blast. We love it.

How did you get into the stocks and commodities business?

It was in 1997. My brother gave me a book by Ken Roberts. A lot of people know Ken Roberts; he's the cowboy-looking guy who was selling the commodity-training course called "The World's Most Powerful Money Manual." That was my first contact with the investment markets. I read that book and became a little interested in that and started to go online, and started communicating with people. And I began to gather money to get more books and then videotapes. Then I just started to become diverse on this subject. I began to get into technical analysis and what investing was about, because it was actually more about futures and commodities before it became centered on stocks and options. To make a long story short, I became a part of this small online community of people. And you know, while you're trading, you're not professionals, so you are free to share different trade ideas. "I'm looking at sugar," or "I'm looking at copper," or "I'm thinking about the S&P."

Well, it just so happened that in the different forums, the trades *we* were putting up were the ones that people were making money on. A lot of people would actually trade them on paper, which means they weren't actually putting their money in them. But they would track them on paper, to follow them and find out whether they were right. If you were buying something, we'd ask whether the market went up. If you were selling something, we'd find out if the market went down. After a while, people were actually putting their money into our recommendations, and the requests came in asking us to put together a free Web site so people wouldn't have to hunt through forums for our different comments. So we did. And it all built from there.

We ended up building a mailing list from that, and actually, the whole payment process began when near the end of 1999 somebody said they wanted to learn how we did it. We weren't even in a position to consider that, but we did think it was flattering.

It was kind of crazy, because then they offered us $5,000. So, as you can imagine, the whole process came together rather quickly for $5,000. That's how the entire process began: The idea of actually charging people for a service came from somebody who loved what they were getting from us for free so much that they were willing to pay if they were able to get more.

It turned out that you really had a knack for doing this kind of trading and people noticed it and wanted to learn from you.

That's exactly right.

So, in part, your success was due to an innate ability. But how do you think you became so good at it?

I would definitely say that it has a lot to do with being gifted in it. But I also think that you can learn how to do it. A lot of people are handicapped in trading because there are so many different ways to look at the markets. There are so many different people that you can listen to, that even if you're pretty good at trading yourself, if you're not confident in your own technical analysis of the market, you can get lost and your ideas can become really clouded. You can become really iffy when you let a lot of other people persuade you otherwise. We weren't like that. We thought, "This is our idea" and that was it. We stuck with it and people saw the confidence and the consistency. People like that. They like dealing with people in this market, and that allows you to know very quickly if somebody's right or wrong, or somebody is confident. A person says, "I'm going to buy this particular market, that's it, I don't care what anybody's saying about this market." That's what makes the market the market. People are buying and people are selling. If everybody were doing the same thing, then the markets wouldn't be what they are. But people like the confidence, and we were acting on our confidence. We were keeping a very consistent track record with people, and they gravitated toward us.

You learned how to do it through your Internet groups, through your online groups, and through reading about it. Did you have a mentor?

No, just books. We read a lot of books and investigated lots of Web sites. It was never a matter of anybody who sat down and said, "OK, I'm going to teach you how to trade, Steve." That never happened.

It was a combination of learning from books and experiencing it and having some natural ability for it.

Right.

People came to you and said, "Will you teach me? I'll pay you." Now you've developed products and a consulting practice to help people do this.

Right, people wanted the technical analysis. Actually, the process of free trade is what started the whole thing because people wanted us to put the trades out for free, and we did that on the Web site. We built the mailing list and at the time that guy offered us $5,000, we had about 1,000 names on our list, which, for us, was pretty big. But, we said to ourselves, why don't we just start a service? And at the time, we charged an outrageous price. It was probably one of the highest-priced services that you were able to get on the Net. We were charging $350 a month to get the charting analysis. We let you pick the three markets that you wanted to get. The work was very, very intensive and it took a lot of time because what happened was, after we did a simple mailing to our list, we had over one hundred people sign up. Think about that—over one hundred people signed up at $350 a month. That was basically, just in cash flow, over $35,000/month! That showed us how powerful the relationship was; we didn't know that the relationships we had were that strong. But it was as simple as printing it up for these clients. We were expecting to get a few people, but we had over one hundred people respond. So that's where our paid service started from—with the chart traders. We then modified it and streamlined it and made things easier on us, while making the information more concise for the end users. And that's where we are today.

You mentioned that the relationships were very strong. To what do you credit that?

Being transparent, you know. We weren't trying to use fanciful language, and people didn't feel as if every time they contacted us, we had a hello and then would give them a pitch, and then say goodbye, or something like that. They didn't feel as if they were being sold, and they got to see that we're real people. They got to experience for free the value of the information that we had. It came to the point where some of them may have felt a certain obligation because they were making money with the free information we were giving them. And, in the investment industry, you can't really fake people out. If you want to try to risk the rules and regulations that come up with some state track record, you go right ahead. But when people are following your trade recommendations in real time, they're going to find out if you're the real deal or not, and that's what happened. Before markets were open, they would see what we were recommending as far as buys and sells, and they would see this day after day, week after week. They would see that this thing was for real, and they were making money. So when we developed our premium service, it was a no-brainer for them to hire us for that.

You had this mailing list and you kept developing your techniques for marketing on the Internet–with stocks and just in general.

Right. We basically started investing and we decided to create our model of charging them for services, and then we went hog wild and started taking revenues we were bringing in from the chart service and investing it in all kinds of Internet marketing courses, and books and strategies. And that's how we started to figure out that there was a lot of garbage out there.

On how to market on the Internet?

Yes, there's more garbage out there than there is gold, believe it or not. Our whole purpose for learning Internet marketing was to build *our* business. It was never our intention, never a twinkle in our eye to think, "We're going to learn Internet marketing so that we can become Internet marketing *teachers*." Plus, we felt as if we were in a tough market. It's one thing to move products in all the "How to Make Money" markets, the ones that say, "You can stay home and make money and do Internet marketing." We're talking about small niche, competitive markets that have money–when you can successfully market online in those kinds of markets, you're pretty good in Internet marketing. We wanted to learn how to do that. So we bought a ton of information on how to do that from people such as Corey Rudl, Jonathan Mizel, Yanik Silver, and Marlon Sanders. We were just buying up that stuff, and I mention them because they have some of the better stuff on the Internet. But we purchased some stuff that wound up being just absolute garbage, too.

You learned along the way what it really took to market on the Internet and be successful?

Right. What happened was, we learned about affiliate programs. We started selling not just our own products and services, but we also began marketing other related and competitive products and services to our list. These were products and services that dealt with investing and trading, stocks and options, futures and commodities. For many of the affiliate programs, we not only became their top affiliate; we also ended up outselling them, and some whole affiliate networks combined. So, of course, that got the attention of the people who wrote the products or owned the services. Then they would e-mail us and say, "Well, what are you doing?" Some people thought their product sucked so bad and that's why they weren't making sales. They'd soon learn that we were making all this money selling their product. It wasn't their product that was poor; it was just that they didn't know what the heck they were doing in terms of marketing online. They would ask us about it and we would tell them what to do. But our focus wasn't on Internet marketing. Eventually, we decided to put together our own product: *Under Oath, The Whole Truth About Internet Marketing.*

So we developed *The Whole Truth* as an e-book. We said, we'll sell at ClickBank.com, give copies for free to the people on our affiliate programs, and we'll be happy if we sell 1,000 copies this year. It was released January 1st...and from January 1st to December

31st, we had already sold over 3,000 copies. We'd reached our goal three times over.

It all developed from what you learned, and from people recognizing that you knew something that they wanted, and out of that came a product.

Absolutely.

And so, now I'm sure everybody that's listening to this will want to know what is *the* secret to Internet marketing. And I'm sure there's not just one secret. But what would you say are the two or three key things that people should know about Internet marketing?

Supply and demand. I think of Ron Popeil. A lot of your audience may be familiar with him; he's a big infomercial guy. He wrote a book called *Salesman of the Century*, and in it he talks about his marketing philosophy, which is: Keep it simple. He talks about his product and how there's a solution to that problem, how much it costs and where to get it, and so on. People don't buy e-books, or teleseminars or seminars; people buy solutions to the problems they have. In other words, when you have a headache and you go to the drugstore, you aren't going to the drugstore to buy some Advil or Excedrin because you think the bottle is sexy and you just want to cuddle it. You're going to find and buy a solution to the pain that's throbbing in your head.

The people who are making the money online are the people who identify markets that have problems for which they have solutions. They package that solution in the form of a book, an e-book, a video series, a cassette series, or a teleseminar. Then they sell that solution to that problem area, basically giving supply to where there's a demand. The money then becomes automatic. There are other things you have to do as far as building the relationship, of course, but supplying a solution to a problem is key. You're not forcing the issue.

You want to make it obvious that this is a solution to your problem and then people would naturally want it, versus having to pound them over the head and say, "Get this."

Right. Because they already know they have a problem. They have a problem and they're looking for a solution. You present the solution. And when you present a solution that's viable, doable, and can help them solve the problem, half your battle's already won.

What about the other half of the battle, having people find you? In your case, you already had a list where people knew of you. How do people who have a solution get themselves out there so people can find them?

Well, we have what we call the "target marketing quadrant," also known as our "four pillars," that generate target and traffic. This deals with search engines, affiliate partners, joint venture partners, and targeted link partners, all of which are absolutely free of charge except for some of the paid inclusion search engines. It's all about targeting your market, knowing exactly who the problem market is, where they're located. Then you have to directly align yourself with that market and with other competitors in that market who can help usher your product to that market.

Joint ventures are an example. We basically have no search engine positioning with *The Whole Truth*, but it was one of the most talked-about products on the Web. On the Alexa rankings, it it was one of the top 2,000 visited Web sites. That happened through setting up joint ventures where people bought the product, loved the product, and then they joint ventured the product and took it to their marketing base. We didn't have the list for Internet marketing because that wasn't our arena. Our customers took it to their marketplace and, because they were well known, that gave our product instant credibility and instant appeal. These were people that the people on their lists already looked up to, admired and respected. When they said, "Look, we highly recommend this product; we purchased it, we've loved it, these are some of the key points you're going to learn, go and check it out for yourself," then everything snowballed from there.

***The Whole Truth* was essentially marketed on joint ventures.**

Absolutely, it was launched on joint ventures, and it continues to thrive on joint ventures and affiliates while having no search engine position.

What is the difference between a joint venture and an affiliate?

An affiliate is somebody who would join your program. They may or may not have the list, and they may purchase some e-zine ads in other people's e-zines, or put a banner on a Web site or a link on their Web site. A joint venture is someone who will grab your product–they'll embrace it, they'll like it, they'll read it, and they'll write an endorsement to their list that's very specific. It is a very direct endorsement of the product and a high recommendation to go to the Web site where it can be purchased.

Under both circumstances, affiliate and the joint venture, they make money off the product. Sometimes, the joint venture product may make more. Because if you're talking about somebody who has a list of 10,000 very strong, active, responsive buyers, or a list of 100,000 OK buyers, either way, you're getting exposure to a market base that you need and don't currently have. What happens is, not only do you get instant buyers, which is instant cash flow for you, you get people to opt-in to your list, which is very important. That is, they may not buy the product now, they may buy it later. These may be people to whom you can start to market other products that are viable to you and that may be viable to them. You can begin to capture their mind and get that mind share that you need so that you can entertain them, if you will. You can build a necessary relationship so that you can start to establish and build your own business.

You're suggesting that one benefit from doing joint ventures is building your list. That way, you can sell your own products to this larger list?

Right. You don't just want to get people to your Web site; you want to get the right people to your Web site. The things you hear about, like guaranteed traffic, that's garbage; it doesn't make sense. What happens is you need to get people to your Web site who have already expressed an interest in what you're selling, and who possibly have the problem that your product is a solution to. One way to do this is by targeting joint ventures.

For us, it was Allen Says of the Warriors Group. All of his people are basically Internet marketers: They look for Internet marketing products and they look for tips and strategies to become better Internet marketers. Allen picked up a copy of our book and he loved it. Then, with a great deal of enthusiasm, he highly recommended it to his list. People just started sledding over to our site, they became affiliates, they purchased the product, and they started linking to us. A ton of different things started to happen at one time.

That's why we tell people, if you have a good product that's already in place, and it solves a problem, but you have zero money to do any advertising, start with joint ventures. It's free, and all you have to do is go to a search engine like Google and start searching in your marketplace. Take those top Web sites, visit their sites, join their mailing lists, observe how they operate, see what kind of offers they put out there, and then present them with your product and how you feel it is a solution to them and to their users. Give them a free preview copy and just start to build a relationship with them because, think about it: People are on the Web to make money. Some people are apprehensive in approaching other Web sites and they think those other sites might be too busy or they may not be interested. But they're actually likely to be looking for other products to sell to their list.

That's a good point. Don't be afraid to contact people; they want to be contacted.

Absolutely. But you can't contact them if it's a lop-sided deal, that is, if it's all about you. They're going to want to know what's in it for them. When you contact them, they have to know that they're not only going to make money off the product, but they're going to look good. Because they're bringing a strong solution-oriented product to their customer base that their customers are going to love and they're going to appreciate. Everybody involved–your targets, their customers, and you (who are presenting the product to them)–everybody is going to be happy and satisfied with the result.

Your Web site, The-Whole-Truth.com, and your e-book, *The Whole Truth*, talks about this, as well as a host of other ways to make money on the Internet.

Right. There are so many different ways that you can market yourself on the Internet–methods that are effective, that are free, and that have been proven to work. We use the concept of "smart money." To try to put it in a nutshell, following the smart money means following the money that knows what it's doing. And with Internet marketing, there are people out there who have already done it, they know what works, and they do it consistently. We don't just buy other people's products. Think about this: Somebody has been on the Internet for 10, 15 years making money. If they put out a product it can cost two hundred bucks; that is, I can invest $200 and learn in a few hours what took them years to learn. You have to respect their wisdom to that extent, where you're willing to make that investment of time to read and study, as well as make the investment money-wise to purchase those products. Because they've done it, they've been there.

We've seen a lot of people doing Internet marketing and they're not making any money. But look at what they're doing–they're submitting things that don't work to FFA (Free Full Access) sites. They're constantly beating their head against the wall trying to figure out how they can make money. They're using classified sites and different things that don't pull in the money; they're just kind of there. They're not doing what the people who are making money online are doing. The easy and simple thing to do is to follow the smart money. This smart money is making money online, and they know exactly what to do, so just emulate what it is they're doing and you can start to build that kind of success too.

That's great advice that makes a lot of sense. Other than following the smart money, what characteristics do you think it takes to be successful in online marketing?

I would say, be realistic. Start with the understanding that success is not about perfection; nothing in life is perfect. Setbacks are inevitable. You need to remember that regardless of how much you put your heart into your business, no matter how badly you want it, and no matter how good your product is, there are going to be setbacks. Setbacks are common, they're inevitable. Not only are they inevitable, they're necessary. But the most important thing is, although they're necessary, they're not supposed to be permanent. They're only temporary. A lot of people may die at the scent of a temporary setback when all they had to do was press on. I think the difference between those who press on and those who don't are those who are more mentally, spiritually, and physically prepared. They know that it's going to happen; they know that a temporary setback is not the end of the world, its just part of the process. Just keep on keeping on. You're going to grow. Hey, fire purifies gold! The fire in your life is supposed to purify you so that you become a better person, you become stronger, and you become wiser. I think that regardless of what you may consider to be the perfect business, regardless of how fantastic your marketing strategies are, you have to understand that nothing in life is perfect and there will be setbacks. Accept it, deal with it, press through it, and everything will be OK.

You're certainly a living example of that, aren't you?

Press and press and press.

Tell us the name of your Web sites for those people who want more information.

There's www.the-whole-truth.com. For our free commodity trades, it's ImpulsiveProfits.com; for chart trader service, it's Charttraders.com. We have a lot of different support Web sites that are free. For those who are interested in learning about Elliot Wave trading, we have Elliott-Wave-Theory.com. For those who are interested in learning about chart formation, we have Future-charts.com. Both of those last two sites are absolutely free. There's no membership required. It's basically a complete online study course. We have about 40 different Web sites that offer support for different things. Many of them have affiliate links on them, in a very subtle way, and that continues to bring in revenue for us. But the whole thing is fun; it's what we love to do. We're extremely motivated, we're enthusiastic about it, and it's just a grand thing. It's a beautiful thing to be able to make money doing what you love to do.

Isn't it, though? I can really hear your joy as you talk about it–that this is really great fun for you.

Yes, it's so much fun. I think it's so true when people say you'll be able to find money and wealth and success doing something that you love to do so much that you would do it for free. Because we were doing this for free. We just expanded recently and started to offer things that were at a premium level for a fee to compensate for our time. But, remember, we started off by giving away free trading information. That's what we were doing.

And you were doing it because you loved doing it.

Right. Somebody came to *us* about pay. It was almost as if, Ding! Oh my gosh! Pay us? Maybe the whole feeling was we didn't deserve to be paid, or we weren't the professionals out there and only the professionals deserved to be paid. But it just goes to show you, people can place a totally different value on you and your information than you may place on yourself.

Others saw a value in what you were doing before you did.

Right.

And the good news is, when you heard it, you opened up and welcomed it and followed that path. In other words, you didn't shut the door when somebody said, "Hey, I'll pay you for this."

Well, actually, when that first person first mentioned it, we kind of cracked the door. But we were thinking, "We don't have a structure!" But when he said, $5,000…$5,000!, we swung that door open so fast that it flew off the hinges.

You were strongly motivated and you took advantage of the opportunity. You said, "Well I don't know exactly how we're going to do it, but let's figure it out."

Absolutely, that's right. We had no structure in place. We had no idea how we were going to do it. But we did it. And it opened up a door to an entire business, and this is where we are today.

What's next for Stephen? Are you going to keep doing this? Do you have other plans, or are you just going to let it keep unfolding as it has been?

Well, we're going to do seminars this summer. We don't plan on doing seminars beyond the ones we've accepted this summer.

We have no plans to put out any other major Internet marketing products. We plan to focus on investing and eventually, to the dismay of many clients, probably, we'll begin to fade out the actual advisory and analysis services, and then just quietly trade on our own in private, with family. We'll retire and go fishing and play video games all day.

And you can, can't you? But currently you stay very busy doing the trading and consulting people on the trade.

Absolutely. Up at 4:00 in the morning, and sometimes don't get to bed until 12:00 midnight.

That's a long day.

Yes it is, but we love what we do. It's not like we dread it, but we're human and we need rest. We need to be able to recuperate, and sometimes we're even working on weekends. But I also enjoy, believe it or not, when 8:00 comes around, so I can sit back in my chair, throw my feet up, and watch Trading Spaces. For some reason, that show relaxes me. So it seems like brief moments of relaxation but they just come and go so quickly.

It sounds as if you want more down time.

Yes, more time to play "Medal of Honor" and "Battlefield." I'm still a big kid, you know.

So, more time to play in general?

Right. More time to play and go bass fishing. I want to go bass fishing not just on a weekend; I want to go bass fishing during a weekday.

And is it that you haven't set up your life to do that yet? Is that what's next, to set up your life so you can?

Exactly. Because the market's open, and then it's almost like a habit, too. When the market's open, I think, Oh, I've got to be there. Clients will email us to say, "OK, I'm out of here, I'm going golfing." Have fun. They're going golfing, I'm not.

What's wrong with that picture?

Right. Yeah, well, they're off and they're golfing, and I'm thinking, geez, why can't I get off? I don't golf, but hey, I'd like to go bowling, or fishing, or learn to golf. Maybe, miniature golf or something.

You want more down time and then with more down time, you'll decide if you need more challenges or something else to do?

I could end up getting more down time and I'd probably say, Nah, I want to go back to the way it was. You get that down time and you kind of miss all the market action and all the interaction with everybody. And I'm still young; I'm 34-years-old.

Yeah, it sounds like what's next for you is striking a balance.

Absolutely. I think I do lack a solid balance between my personal life and business life. I have allowed myself to become very consumed. With success, you're constantly moving, it's constantly flowing. I don't think there's an actual destination; I think it's an evolutionary process where you're constantly growing, expanding and learning, adjusting, and this is where we are in our particular phase. Because once this is adjusted, there's going to be something else.

That's right. I'm delighted that you said that because it echoes what I believe: You never arrive, it's always about what there is to learn next or do differently next, or whatever the next challenge is–for all of us.

Don't ever think you have arrived. I mean, think about it. If you're there, if you're at that pinnacle and you think that's it, then there's only one other place to go. If you can't maintain it, it's going to go down. What's going to motivate you to keep on going if you've reached that destination? Success isn't a peak where you come up one side of the mountain and then go down the other side. It's constantly, forever moving. It's like a river; it constantly just flows and moves.

Do you have any parting advice for anyone who wants to market their business or products on the Internet or to pursue their dreams in any other way?

I would say, out of everything, know that your financial independence is dependent on other people, so do good by other people. And, remember, somebody who will talk evil to you about somebody is just as capable of talking evil about you to somebody else. You have to watch your associations–the people you allow yourself to be associated with. Don't allow yourself to be associated with those who will tear you down. It's the stuff you always hear–believe in yourself, you can do it, but really, you actually can't do it alone.

There's nothing in my particular background that says I should be where I am today. If you look at a lot of other people who are successful, it's the same thing. You have to be consistent and know that things are going to happen that will set you back and they're going to upset you, they're going to irritate you. But that's just a part of being an entrepreneur. I mean, if it was easy, everybody would be wealthy, everybody would be rich, everybody would be an entrepreneur, nobody would be working 9-5, there would be no one at the gas station, no one at McDonald's. So understand that being an entrepreneur is being a unique being. Entrepreneurs are a very small, elite group of people, and to be a part of that elite group of people, it requires something very special on the inside that goes well beyond just desiring something. You can sit back and desire it all you want, but your desire is going to be tested. That's where you're going to have to show how determined you are. You have to be able to press on in the face of adversity, in the face of a setback. You have to be able to think on your feet, to think outside of the box. Be unique. Be creative. And you'll just continue to move, continue to flow. Pace yourself. It doesn't have to be a 100-yard dash. Be a long distance runner. Just pace yourself and keep moving toward places you want to go, and just have fun. I mean, really, it's about just doing it, and doing it consistently and having fun in the process. If you're not enjoying it while you're in the process of doing it, then you might as well not do it.

Great advice. Stephen, thanks so much for being with us, and for sharing all this valuable information. I know that people are going to get a lot from it.

I hope they do, Stacey, and I appreciate you having me. Again, I don't consider myself to be a speaker; I'm not a guru of any kind.

I am a regular person just like the next one. I was persistent though; I remained persistent and consistent, and congruent in the different things that we do to market online. I think that if we can do it, anybody can do it, regardless of what's in his or her background. Anybody can do it.

That's really inspiring.

Well thank you.

Thank you!

Three Key Success Principles Plus Coaching Questions and Action Steps

Stephen Pierce

Key Success Principle #1:

Strengthen Your Relationships:

Your Financial Independence Is Dependent Upon Your Connections to Others

Many people think of the day when they will be financially independent as "freedom day." And, while financial independence is a worthwhile goal, it does not mean that you are free of your dependence on other people. As a matter of fact, in order to create financial independence, you just might need a lot more people in your life than you have right now. Financial independence, as we are defining it here, means having streams of income that cover all the bills and which are not dependent on the number of hours you work.

Let's look at it from both a vendor and customer perspective. Being financially independent requires building a well-oiled machine or a system that continuously produces income (assuming that you did not inherit your money). Once you have built that well-oiled machine, you will need people to keep that system running–competent people you can trust.

Secondly, the income stream must be coming from somewhere; i.e., someone must be purchasing whatever it is you are selling or your investments must continuously be producing a return. For people to buy, they must trust that what you are selling is a viable product and that you are a viable entity. They may not know you personally, but they need to have a strong relationship with you and/or your business to buy from you and to send other customers your way.

How Stephen Built Relationships:

Stephen built relationships with a community of people online. He originally shared his knowledge free of charge. Then people asked him to create a Web site where they could access his specific information for free. He willingly did it. People followed his suggestions and found him to be competent and trustworthy. Eventually someone recognized Stephen's talent and offered to pay him good money to teach him how to trade more successfully. They saw value in what Stephen did before he recognized it himself. That was because Stephen had built credibility by consistently performing well.

Once he had a product to offer, he already had that credibility with a large list of people. This became a ready-made customer base, one that consisted of relationships he had built over time.

Coaching Questions:

1) How are your relationships with clients? Competitors? Potential prospects? Employees? Vendors? Neighbors?

2) How do each of them view you?

3) Which relationships would you like to strengthen?

Call to Action:

1) Choose a person or group of people with whom you would like to build stronger relationships.

2) Make a conscious effort to connect with these people over the coming weeks.

3) Intend to become the kind of person you would want to do business with and/or be in a relationship with.

Key Success Principle #2

Develop Your Resilience Muscle: Bounce Back from Setbacks

Resilience is the art of bouncing back from setbacks. When you have a setback, you can either: a) swim around in the muck, feel sorry for yourself, and beat yourself up, or b) acknowledge the setback and the feelings you have about it, learn from it, and redirect your course as needed and move forward.

The truth is that you will have setbacks along the way. This is just inevitable. The sooner you accept that, the better. Many of these setbacks will take the form of circumstances that come up and block your way. If you look closely, you may find these setbacks are directly correlated with your innermost thoughts, fears, and limiting beliefs. This is because we create what we focus on including those things we don't want. (See Special Section with Dr. Van Tharp for a more in-depth discussion of this principle.)

Don't get stopped by these bumps in the road; learn from them. As you work through the setbacks that come up, you will become the person you need to be to live out your dreams.

How Stephen Bounced Back from Setbacks:

Stephen never let go of his dream of being an entrepreneur despite many failures he had along the way. He bounced back from some big setbacks including dropping out of high school and declaring bankruptcy.

One of the things he learned along the way is that it is okay to be different. Stephen realized that many entrepreneurs are non-conformists. He learned to let go of what other people thought and to be his own person. This is an important lesson. Entrepreneurs don't succeed because they fit in. They succeed in part because they bring something new and unique to what they do.

Stephen learned to expect setbacks and know they are temporary and that he must "press on." "Pressing on" led to creating a career he loves *and* becoming a millionaire.

Coaching Questions:

1) How easily do you get stopped in life?

2) Do you view setbacks as permanent or temporary?

Call to Action:

1) Choose to adopt a philosophy that views all setbacks as temporary.

2) Take a look at the last setback you had. What can you learn from it? Make a decision that moves you forward based on what you learned.

Key Success Principle #3

Form Creative Alliances:
Invite in New People and Opportunities

If you want to grow big without suffering burnout, you will need the help of others. One way to do this is to form alliances. Even your competitors can become allies if you find a way for them to win too.

In today's world of high-speed communications, your allies can be located anywhere–from right next door to across the globe. Your allies can market your business for you and share in the profits, or they can take on portions of the work that you are not interested in doing, or you can co-create a joint project with your allies. Be willing to look outside yourself. Having more than one person in the mix sparks new and creative ideas. Stephen Covey, author of *Seven Habits of Highly Successful People,* defines synergy as: One plus One is equal to or greater than Three.

How Stephen Formed Alliances:

Stephen's e-book, *The Whole Truth,* was sold entirely via his email list and the lists of his allies. He formed joint ventures and brought on affiliates who liked his book, believed in it, and wanted to sell it to their list of contacts. In return, they got a percentage of the profits. As a result, Stephen's e-book sold at triple the expected rate without ever being listed on a search engine.

Coaching Questions:

1) How could alliances help you grow?

2) Where could you most benefit from having alliances?

Call to Action:

1) Write down the names of people or groups or types of people with whom you would most like to form an alliance.

2) Create a win-win proposal from which all parties would benefit.

3) Contact the people on your list and offer the proposal. Let them know how they could win from it.

My Key Learnings from This Chapter:

1)

2)

3)

Chapter #6:
John Dessauer

Real Estate Investor and Business Owner

*Escapes the Rat Race to Save His Family
and Becomes a Multi-Millionaire
in Two Years*

Chapter 6

· · · · · · · · · · · ·

John Dessauer
Real Estate Investor, Business Owner,
and Multi-Millionaire

> *"When you engage in systematic, purposeful action, using and stretching your abilities to the maximum, you cannot help but feel positive and confident about yourself."*
>
> – Brian Tracy

I am here today with John Dessauer. John is founder and president of the Dessauer Group; he is a real estate investor specializing in multi-family units and has become a multi-millionaire through real estate investing.

Tell us John, how long have you been investing in real estate?

Since we got our first property, it's been 2 ½ years.

OK, and in that time, how much have you accumulated in real estate assets?

We've done phenomenally well in the last 2½ years. We've acquired about $30,000,000 in real estate, and that's even hard for *me* to believe. It has been a whirlwind in those 2½ years. I know that that's a lot of acquisitions to have made, but the most important factor was the way that we made them, and even more important than that was why we made those acquisitions. We had a strong will to succeed in real estate investing because of what it offers, and we still have that desire. We're consistently looking at new real estate, and at offers and properties and deals. There's no stopping us now. Even though we've gone to that level, we are just so enticed and interested and pleased and excited about real estate investing that I don't know what level we're going to climb to, but it's going to be really big. It's already big, but it's going to get bigger.

Let's talk about why you got involved in real estate. What were you doing prior to that?

My story was that of like many other people–my wife and I met in college and after college, we ended up getting married and having two kids. We were pursuing the American dream, and we found ourselves in a situation at eight or nine years into our marriage, where what had happened with our relationship scared us, and we changed some things in our relationship and in our lives, and it's made an unbelievable difference.

Up until that point, I was doing sales for a company, doing fairly well, and had progressed through my career from graduating college to slowly moving up the ladder. Because we were striving for that All-American Dream, we had the house in the suburbs, the two cars, and all of that. My wife, Rhonda, had a job where she was running a restaurant, so she would leave about 4:00 in the afternoon and be gone till 1:00, 2:00, 3:00 in the morning. That's the restaurant business. And, of course, I was gone during the day from 7:00 in the morning until 5:00 or 6:00 at night. We found ourselves doing that for about eight years and, in that time frame, we were like two ships passing in the night. We really fell out of familiarity with each other. We went from being best friends to not knowing who that other person was.

It came to a point where she felt that the love wasn't there, and we were going to go our separate ways. Well, that bit of news hit me like a ton of bricks. I reacted a little bit differently than she did but I just couldn't fathom any notion of only seeing my kids one, two days a week. That was not going to work for me and I knew at that point there were big issues and we were in trouble. I just didn't know how much we were being affected, and why.

Because we were working those types of schedules, and because we had a high amount of debt, what we call today bad debt, we were almost slaves to the situation we were in. We had to keep our jobs, and we had to work hard and make sure the money was coming in. But when that news came to me, when she felt that we needed to go our separate ways and the love wasn't there anymore, that was a real awakening for me. I realized at that point that everybody who told me anything about what I needed to do with my career in order to progress—as far as go to school, get a good job, a good car—it just wasn't working. I immediately decided that I had to make some changes, not only to myself, but so those changes would eventually reach my family and give me an opportunity to save what I had. I started looking at different ways of how I would receive income, such as starting my own business, investing in real estate—some other ways that you receive income differently from what I was doing at the time. I wanted to somehow get more time where I could work on mending my family, be creative with new businesses, win my wife back, all that good stuff. I thought that would be the ticket not only to financial freedom but really to a life freedom that I was searching for. I decided at that point I was going to receive and earn income differently, and that's why I started to look into real estate.

You went into real estate to save your marriage and to save your family.

Yes, and that was really my reason why; that was my fuel for doing anything. As I look back on it today and think about what we have acquired and accomplished and what we continue to accomplish, it just makes me believe that the fuel was so strong and there was such a large amount of it that it was never ending and that's why we have been able to do what we have done in the last 2 ½ years. The moment we started to receive income differently from our real estate investments, by that I mean receive income without expending our time, my relationship with my wife and kids changed. Additionally, I was able to have the time to create other businesses and just really enjoy life and have fun. It's been a true blessing.

When you were making the transition, how did you go about learning how to do real estate?

It was a total submersion of everything and anything that had to do with real estate–whether it was sitting down and talking with someone who owned property, or going to seminars and buying CD's and tapes, and reading books–you name it. I was fascinated with it all once I learned about leverage. This meant that I, or anyone, could get into it with very little money.

We hear so much about offers that require "no money down." Real estate does provide the opportunity to make investments with little or no money down. Because of our situation financially, which at the time was a wreck, I was enticed by real estate because it was something that I could get into with little or no money down. That was the first thing that enticed me. Then I started to learn about leverage–not only using other people's money to buy real estate, but also using other people's time, and I'll give you an example. You buy a four-unit building; those four tenants in that building go to their 9 to 5's. They spend their time to cut you what is (to them) the most important check of the month.

I saw that, and I had to be a part of that. I could see where I could buy that investment, use other people's money to buy it, use other people's time to pay for it, and by using other people's knowledge, to learn how to get into that, I felt that I could totally maximize my leverage because I didn't have a lot of that. I didn't have a lot of the knowledge; I didn't have a lot of the money. I actually didn't have any money, but I did have a lot of time on my hands to learn about this subject–because when I sat down with Rhonda at that point and we had that conversation, the next day I went in and quit my job. For me, it was sink or swim, do or die. I had to succeed at real estate, I had to do it on a large scale, and I felt that by using all those different types of leverage, I was going to be able to not only succeed, but succeed in a big way. It was just going to take one thing required on my end, and that was taking action. That's never been a problem for me; I've always been an action-type guy. I knew if I could take action, I could use that leverage and do some wonderful things with it.

You quit your job cold turkey?

I quit my job cold turkey, and as I tell people when I'm speaking from stage, when you're going through a marriage issue, that's not the best thing that your wife wants to hear–that you just quit your job. But I felt that if I was going to sacrifice my family for my career or a job that I thought was only OK, not anything I enjoyed, it wasn't worth it. I knew that I could change what I was doing, I knew that I could change my life, and when I came home and told her that I quit my job, it was like pouring gasoline on a fire.

But sometimes you have to create damage to heal yourself. I know that sounds kind of strange, but I think that's the whole premise behind surgery, for example. A surgeon has to cut you open and actually create damage to make the whole individual better, and that's the way I looked at it. I knew my situation was probably going to get worse before it got better, but once it started to get better, I had no fears about what I had done, and my confidence slowly began to build. I took baby steps just like you would come out of surgery and take small steps to recover. It made all the difference in the world approaching it like that.

So, yes, I did quit my job, quit it cold turkey, and I certainly don't recommend anybody just go out and quit his or her job. But for my situation, it was something that I thought I had to do. It's really worked out to be the absolute best decision I've probably ever made.

I want to back up a minute. You started talking about leverage, and just by virtue of the fact that you invest in multi-unit apartments, that is taking leverage to another level, isn't it?

Yes. As I started to look into real estate, one of the things that I did not want to create was another job for myself. Remember, I had a family to mend; I had a relationship to mend, and I did not want to create another 9 to 5 for myself. I learned the rules about leverage and understood how you can take leverage, and accomplish a lot with very little. I continued to look at that aspect in my real estate investing, not only to acquire the property, but I also looked at that aspect on the types of properties that I was going to acquire. As I compared single-family houses to multi-unit apartment buildings, one thing I noticed was that I could again apply that rule of leverage with multi-unit apartment buildings; the transactions are very similar.

The time frames and the steps are similar to close on a ten-unit building and to close on a single-family house. If I could do ten times as much revenue from a ten-unit building than a single-family house, that would be a benefit. If I could have ten people going to their 9 to 5's to cut me the most important check of the month, rather than earn one myself, I saw that as a benefit. Once you own multi-family unit properties, I think there's more leverage that you can apply to increase value on them. I looked at multi-family units as a focus to my investing. I still invest in single-family homes, but I tend to focus more on multi-family unit housing.

You can do one closing versus ten closings and make the same as you would on, perhaps, ten individual homes, is that right?

Absolutely, and not only the closing aspect. If I bought a ten-unit building, I still close one time but I have ten units, yet the costs are a lot less. If I'm looking at ten units in one building or ten single-family houses, and I want to close on those ten units on both sides, I've got closing costs, appraisal costs, not to mention the costs to find the properties. But once I own them, if I'm going to check up on my ten units, I can go to one building, check on all ten units, and be out of there within 20 minutes. If I look at ten single-family houses, I may have to go to ten parts of a single city, or maybe separate cities to check on my investments. It was not only a money issue as far as leverage, but it was certainly a time issue. Again, I had a family to mend. I wanted to maximize that opportunity to start dealing with that, rather than create a job for myself where all my time would be eaten up with the property management of my investment.

Did you start with a ten-unit building, or did you start smaller?

I started with a duplex. The reason that I liked the duplex was that once I got it, it eliminated completely all the negativity that had begun to plague me. I was getting into this, and as is so common, the negative thoughts began. I'd think, "John, what if you buy this and the tenants move out?" or "What if you buy this and someone trashes the place?" I started to ask myself those types of questions that create fear. What I've learned through that process is that we are creatures of habit—we create our own fear through the questions that we ask ourselves.

I've also learned with that process that if I want to diminish fear, I need to ask myself different questions. I ask myself empowering questions. I might ask myself a complete opposite question than I would typically ask myself. Here's an example. Instead of asking myself, "What if I buy this building and all the tenants move out?" I turn that question around and ask, "What if I buy this building and I don't have any turnover for five years in tenants?" Then I would come across another problem, such as "Do I raise rents every year?" If I ask those opposite questions, they may spark more thought, but what they do is eliminate and definitely reduce any fear that you have.

I use that process today when I'm looking at a 300-unit complex—the same principle applies. I did start small, I started with a duplex, and we just really took off from there. It's been wonderful.

We still own the duplex, by the way, and I would suggest that anybody getting involved in real estate investing should start small, take baby steps, and you'd be surprised how fast you go from there. It's like a snowball rolling downhill; it does start small, but if you're rolling down a hill in snow, that thing will grow significantly.

You talked about some fears that people have about investing in real estate, such as tenants moving out or damage to the property, or that kind of thing. Have you come up against the realities of that?

Yes, we have. You are going to come across situations that are somewhat challenging, that are going to be hurdles in front of you. There are a lot of late-night guys on TV who present a rosy picture of real estate investing–you know, sitting by the side of the beach or the pool and talking about success with real estate. I'm here to tell you a little bit different story than that.

You are going to have some challenges. There are going to be tenants who move out on you. There are going to be tenants who aren't the best fit for that property, or a fit for any property, for that matter. You're going to come across those, and if you use good judgment, good sound skills and property management, you will take a positive and fearless approach. You can do some wonderful things. If you have a strong enough reason to do so, you can roll right through those challenges, over those hurdles, and believe it or not, you're able to turn those challenges into opportunity. You're able to turn those challenges into something of a positive nature, rather than a negative nature. That's how I look at things now. For real estate investors who are just getting into it, they need to be prepared to experience some challenges with their investing. As long as they know that up front, they should be able to deal with anything that comes along.

So you see what is possible in a situation instead of expecting it will be terrible, and then if some obstacle does arise, you approach it as providing an opportunity?

That's right. You may have a tenant who's a bad tenant, and you need to get them out of there, but maybe it's an opportunity, not only to get them out of there, but maybe you increase the rent by $10 or $15 for the next tenant who moves in for instance. I typically look at situations that are negative and try to work with them to turn their circumstances into something positive with my real estate investing. It eliminates the fear when I make investments today.

Great. We discussed earlier that you jumped cold turkey into this career. But along the way you've learned how to leverage your risk by means of using formulas or measurements, and you've developed other ways to help you determine whether something is a good investment or not. Will you say a bit more about this?

I use a set of ratios that help me when I'm looking at property, but most importantly, to reduce risk, I surround myself with a good team. I have an attorney who I work with; I have my accountant and bookkeeper. We started our property management company so I do not have to deal with leaky faucets or things like that. I include my insurance agent and some other people who are key to reduce risk. So, number one, and most importantly, to reduce my risk, I have a team in place.

And, on the other side, I basically use four ratios. I look at them continually to give me an advantage when I'm looking at property. Those four are the following:

Number one is the capitalization rate, which is a ratio of the performance of the property to sales price. It shows a financial performance for the property.

Number two is cash return on investment, which is how well my investment that I put down on the deal, if any, is doing.

The third ratio is very similar to the second one. It's a total cash return on investment, which is a more precise picture of how well the money that I pulled out of my pocket to make that investment is performing for me.

Finally, the fourth ratio is the debt service coverage ratio. That's a ratio that shows how well that property is going to service the debt that's against it. The bank really looks at that one and relies on that one pretty heavily.

If you look at those four ratios, and you understand them, and the numbers work out using those, and you have a good team behind you, you can do some wonderful things with real estate investing with respect to your bank and making creative offers, and doing creative financing.

But, primarily, you've got to have the knowledge in those four ratios, and after that, you've got to take the action step of realizing that you can't do anything alone with respect to real estate investing. You must have a team behind you. With those two things, you've really become a pretty important and strong force with your real estate investing. It also eliminates, or at least reduces, a lot of risk that you take with that investment.

Great. So, how could people learn more about those ratios?

Since going through this process, I've realized what it's done for me, with my family and financials. I've kept my paper trail so I could share this with people and show others how I did what I did and how I continue to do what I do. We also started a seminar

company, The Dessauer Group; our Web site is
www.TheDessauerGroup.com. We've got a series of seminars and
products that teach those four ratios, but also property
management, making creative offers, and different topics that help
people acquire that first leg out of the three legs of leverage. They
start to acquire the knowledge so that they can eliminate some of
the other hurdles they may come across, such as lack of confidence,
and lack of money.

I would also recommend general reading. There are so many
people who are writing books about real estate investing. It is
valuable to go to seminars and talk with as many people as you
can about what real estate investing is and what it takes to be
successful at it.

**With more knowledge, you not only lower your risk, but
you build your confidence level.**

Yes. It seems that the first thing that comes into people's minds
when they think of real estate investment is, "I can't do that, I
don't have the money." The next thing that comes into people's
minds is, "I would be afraid to get involved in that because of
everything I've ever heard about tenants." So, in general, people
back away from it from a lack of confidence. What I've found
through this whole process is that there are three hurdles to cross,
and those are two of them.

The final hurdle is a lack of knowledge. People think, "I can't
invest in real estate; I just don't know how to do it." What I found
through this whole transformation is that if you take care of one
of those hurdles, the other two will resolve automatically. That
most fundamental hurdle to cross is a lack of knowledge. If you
acquire the knowledge, you can eliminate the lack of money and
the lack of confidence. If you know how to make creative offers

and buy real estate with little or no money down, you eliminate the lack of money. If you had all the money in the world, or had the opportunity to buy all the property that you wanted in the world, or at least a lot of it, with little or no money down, you would have quite a bit of confidence about you. It starts with the knowledge that you have to *obtain* the knowledge, and that eliminates the other two obstacles. It's like a magic trick.

What are the biggest mistakes you see new investors making?

That's a great question. Well, I think the first mistake is the fact that they do not surround themselves by a team, number one. I think number two, is that they try to go after bigger properties than they should begin with. The reason you want to start small is because you are going to have hurdles and mistakes that you go through. When they're smaller hurdles, smaller mistakes, you can get by those quite a bit easier than if they were large mistakes. People who buy some of these larger investments have mistakes without the proper knowledge or experience. They tend to find themselves buried, and it typically can ruin them–and not just for a long time, actually forever. So, those are two big ones.

I think the most important mistake that investors make is that they never take action. They say they're investors, but they don't own any property. They say they're investors, and they might have one property, but they don't have the wherewithal or have not taken the action steps to put themselves in a position where they can buy a second piece of property.

Those are mistakes that I see quite often. By surrounding yourself with a good team and starting small, and continuing to take action, you tend to grow fast. You tend to get by some of the mistakes and hurdles, and find yourself in a position where it's like that snowball running downhill–the bigger it gets, and the faster it rolls downhill, the less work that you put into it and it seems to grow without effort.

You've mentioned having a team twice now. That is a process in itself. What has helped you find the right team members?

It is a process. As you can tell by our little conversation here, I tend to talk quite a bit, although I'm also a good listener. When I started out, I must have talked to everybody and their mother. I wanted to know what everybody was doing in real estate investing; I wanted to know how they did it, I wanted to know how long it took them to do it, and as I started talking to more people, specific names would come up.

When I was talking to someone that worked at a title company, or a real estate broker, or someone that owned property, a particular attorney's name kept coming up. I knew that was someone I should get in touch with. So, the best way to start identifying team members is to start talking and ask questions. It's a wonderful way to learn, and you'll be alert to names that come up continually, whether it's an attorney, an accountant, a real estate broker, or an insurance person. I would suggest that you sit down with those people, tell them your game plan, tell them why you're investing in real estate or want to get involved in real estate, and find out what they're all about.

You might want to look at it as a type of interview process. Once that's completed and you're comfortable with that person, then you have that person in place. You need to make sure you utilize that person. A team is very important, and I would say the best way to start looking for team members is to talk with as many people as you can and ask questions.

Have you found that your team has evolved and changed over time or have you stuck with the same team?

I've got some team members who have been there from the beginning; they're wonderful, and I've found that they've learned a lot of things. Even though they're very specialized and do what they do, one should never stop learning. I look for people who know that they don't know it all–they know a good portion of it, but they're eager to learn, they're eager to adapt. I've had some other team members whom I've had to let go. I say no hard feelings, but I'm on a mission here, and you don't really play in the plans for that mission. It's nothing personal, I like you as a friend, but as far as a business decision, someone on my team, I really have to feel comfortable with that person in terms of my mission.

When people present themselves where they're not part of that team, you've got to relinquish them from that relationship. You've got to separate them and bring somebody in who is eager to work for you, who wants to take action, who understands your reason why, and is ready to rock and roll.

You may go through a process where you eliminate a few people from your team. You are going to have some people who are going to be "on" from the beginning, and it makes for a nice mix, but everything should be evolving and adapting to the situation, and that's how I want my team members to be in place, where they consistently evolve and take action, and learn new things. We move forward as a group.

John, you said in the beginning that you wanted to keep going even though you've been as successful as you have. How do you think you grew so fast and mended your family at the same time?

Good question. Well, I would say that I started to mend my family from a principle that I think a lot of people hear all the time when they're flying. When the flight attendant is announcing the safety precautions on a flight, they'll tell you to first put the oxygen mask on yourself so that you can help other people around you. So many times when people get caught up in life, they tend to want to put the oxygen mask on everybody else, and I kind of found myself with that situation. I tried to change my wife, my boss, everybody around me. I never looked to change and improve on myself. The moment that I started to do that, it made all the difference in the world with the people around me. By changing myself, I truly changed everybody around me.

That started with my different mindset and outlook with real estate investing, with my career. I made the commitment to myself that instead of taking responsibility for my life, I was going to take charge of my life. I didn't want to get caught up in just making a living; rather, I wanted to design a life for my family and me. When I started to buy real estate, people could already see the changes in me, most notably my wife.

After I started to buy real estate, I changed some other aspects of my life, and her interest peaked. That drew us from being strangers to thinking, "Hey, well, what's going on with you here? You seem different." We began to get to know each other again. I was somewhat of a new person, but yet the same old Johnny D. but with some new standards. I became a new-and-improved Johnny D.

We started to buy real estate creatively. I can think of some closings where we actually got checks back at closing; we didn't have to put any money down. Rhonda took quite a liking to that. In her thinking it went from being a crazy, hairball scheme, to something that would work in a big way. We began to see that this would work to have this money coming in whether we go to our

9 to 5's or not. We thought we can use that time, not only to rekindle what we had and become best friends again, but to start new businesses, be creative, maybe coach a couple of basketball teams with our kids.

There are so many things you can do when you have that freedom. It's a lot of fun today. I absolutely adore my wife, we're best friends, and we have a great relationship with our kids. We're able to do things that I know other people can't do, and it's because we set ourselves up to do that. It was the real estate investing that provided the freedom of time. I think that I get paid in time now rather than money. It's just worked out wonderfully.

It sounds as if you have developed strategies–you learned a lot from other people, and you've developed some of your own strategies, such as ways to get money back at closing. Is that right?

Absolutely. I really attribute it to my situation at the time. There are so many people who teach real estate investing and creative real estate investing and all of that, but they don't teach the premise of having a strong enough reason for getting involved in it. My reasoning was such a motivator that I couldn't simply get involved in real estate investing, buy one property, and go back to my regular life. I had to keep going. To do that, I had to take what I learned, and identify new ideas, new creative things that would enable me to create value, pull that new value out, and buy more property.

There are a lot of techniques that I picked up and learned and do today that enable me to buy property with very little money down. I took quite a few ideas from people I'd learned from, but I also developed a lot on my own. I had no idea whether they would work or not, but I had to try it because I didn't have the money at the time. I had to take it to the next level of creative real estate investing, so I did create a lot. I'm really proud of what we've created. I see people whom I get involved with now do wonderful things with their real estate investing. It really pleases me. You can actually take something that is a negative in your life, and make it a wonderful thing. When you pass that on to other people, they're able to change their lives and do some wonderful things, and it's a great feeling.

You now teach some of the strategies you've developed in your real estate courses.

Absolutely. They're strategies having to do with buying the property—how to get in that property with absolutely no money down; some credits that we use include rent credits, security deposit credits, deferred maintenance credits; and taking cash reserves at closing. There are so many different ways that you can eliminate, or at least reduce the amount you're putting down on a property, and that's really all I'm concerned about. If I have a $100,000 property, and I know I have to put down 20%, all I'm concerned about as far as getting creative, is that 20%. I don't try to tackle the whole thing; I just try to tackle the 20%. That makes it more of a palatable challenge, and there are so many ways you can reduce that 20%. It's actually fun when you start getting into properties and situations and things like that.

Once you own the property, you can also use several different creative ways to increase value—pull that new value out—so that you can buy more property. There are techniques such as the one that I call "divide and conquer" which is really almost like buying a whole case of pop at the store for $7 or $8, but if you go to a vending machine, you can buy individual cans for $1 or more. Now, nothing's changed with the drinks; the only thing that has changed is the packaging. What I learned with my real estate is that if I change the packaging, I change the value. I have learned and I teach those kinds of things on a daily basis, but more importantly, I use them on a daily basis–not only to buy property, but also to increase value so that I can pull that out and go buy more. Using those techniques is the main reason why I've grown to this level in such a short amount of time.

In parting, what is one piece of advice for anyone considering real estate or making a basic life change?

If they're considering real estate, or considering a life change, I think I have to really go back to the importance of taking care of you first. If you don't take care of yourself, there's never a chance to take care of those around you. You have to make that decision, and you've got to make that a commitment to yourself. On the surface, it may sound somewhat selfish, but it's probably the deepest, most commitment-minded thing you can do for the people who surround you.

I would also say that you have to establish your "why." You have to truly fuel what you do and how you do it. You need to have that motivating factor. Once you have that why, I typically tell my students to post that in three spots–on their bathroom mirror (so they see that whenever they get up in the morning and when they go to bed at night), their car visor (so they see that when they get into and out of their automobile), and then thirdly, in one more place of high visibility–at your desk at work, on your TV or remote control, a treadmill, wherever you spend a lot of time.

They should establish their goals, but I don't want their goals to be a motivating factor for them. Goals need to be stair steps–they need to be accomplished and arranged, but then move on to the next goal. So many times we let our goals motivate us, and our goals aren't motivating. But our reason why is. I want you to identify your goals; I want you to write them down so you're taking them from the mental to the physical, and then put them away for six months. I guarantee that if you put three to five goals away for six months, and you let your reason why fuel you, you are going to do some wonderful things. When you look at them in six months, you will be flabbergasted of what you've accomplished. That would be the second step.

So, number one is to take care of yourself. Number two; write down your goals and your reason why. The third step may be one of the most important things that you can do along with the other two. There's really no level of importance here; they're all important. You have to take action. So many people will do the first two steps and they won't take action at all. Being in action is just as important as the other two. Be in action and do it now. You can't be a procrastinator and say, "I'm going to take action tomorrow."

An analogy is that sign you'll see at some bars sometimes that says, "Free beer tomorrow." You know, I show up there tomorrow, and that sign's still there, "Free beer tomorrow." So, there's never a point where there's free beer today. You've got to take that action today.

To wrap up, if you do those three things, you're going to get some wonderful results, whether it's to change your life, buy real estate, develop a new business, change a relationship, whatever that is. You're going to do some wonderful, wonderful things.

Great, thank you so much, John.

Three Key Success Principles Plus Coaching Questions and Action Steps

John Dessauer

Key Success Principle #1:

You Take Some, You Give Some:

When You Leverage Time, Knowledge and Money, You'll Skyrocket to Success

One person can only do so much in the number of hours in a given day. Leverage is about using resources such as time, money and knowledge in such a way that it expands your capabilities beyond your own internal resources. In the previous chapter, we talked about building allies; this is one form of leverage.

Each of us has a limited amount of time, knowledge and/or liquid cash. When you find ways to use other people's time, knowledge or money, you expand your capacity to grow. Below are just a few examples of ways to do this:

To leverage your time, you can find other people who can perform some of the time-consuming activities, choose products that give a greater return for the amount of time invested, create residual streams of income that require a large amount of time upfront but very little down the road, or partner with others who will do the legwork in return for your investment of money.

To leverage knowledge, you can create a team of people, each of whom has specialized knowledge in a specific area. These people can be employees or entrepreneurs or even owners of larger businesses. You can also hire a mentor, attend workshops or classes, etc.

To leverage money, you can borrow money from a bank, individual investors, or other sources; or form a joint venture where a partner gets a portion of the profits in return for their investment.

How John Uses Leverage:

John learned to leverage money, knowledge and time. Initially, the biggest resource he had was time. So he leveraged money to purchase his first duplex and leveraged knowledge by attending all the workshops on real estate he could, and built a strong team of experts he could rely on.

In buying multiplexes, he leverages time and money. He leverages the tenants' money to pay the mortgage. He leverages time because he only has to visit one property and do one closing while earning income from multiple units.

Coaching Questions:

1) Which do you have the most of: time, knowledge or money?

2) How can you use that resource to your advantage?

3) Which do you have the least of: time, knowledge or money?

4) Who has that resource and how can you leverage it?

5) Who do you need on your team to balance your strengths and shore up your weaknesses?

Call to Action:

1) Make a list of all the ways you can leverage your resources. Do some research through the Internet and people you know to find the people who can most help you in this area.

Key Success Principle #2

Headed to the Doghouse or the Penthouse?
Ask Yourself the Most Empowering Questions

Most people ask themselves all the wrong questions–questions such as: *What's wrong with me? Why did I do that?* These are questions that cause you to look backward. They serve no purpose other than to beat yourself up and to keep you stuck exactly where you are.

Another type of disempowering question casts a negative projection on the future. These are questions such as*: What if I fail? What if they say no?* These questions cause you to focus on the worst-case scenario. Usually the answers to these questions aren't as bad as we make them out to be. A more empowering thing to do is flip the question around. *What if I succeed? What if they say yes?* If you have a fear of success, the answers to these questions can also be scary, but then you can look realistically at how to deal with success.

The most empowering questions cause your mind to look into the future and seek the solution to a problem. Examples are: *How could I do this despite this obstacle? Who could help me with this? I wonder what other choices I have. How* and *who* questions are generally more empowering.

It is also helpful to "wonder" about a subject. Wondering is about being curious. Using this word may help you lighten up as opposed to feeling like you have to find an answer immediately. Try using those words right now about something that has you feeling stuck– *"I wonder how this will turn out"* or *"I wonder what my next step should be"* or *"I wonder …"*.

How John Asked Himself Empowering Questions:

John said, "We create our own fear through the questions that we ask ourselves." He learned to diminish fear by asking himself different questions. Instead of asking, "What if I buy this building and all the tenants move out?" he turns that question around and asks, "What if I buy this building and I don't have any turnover in tenants for five years?" Then he would come across another problem, such as, "Do I raise rents every year?" John found that if he asked those opposite questions, they might spark more thinking, but they definitely reduced any fear that he had. He uses the same process when buying much larger multiplex properties today.

Coaching Questions:

1) In what situations do you feel the most fear?

2) Think about those situations now. What questions are you asking yourself? Are they empowering or disempowering questions?

3) What is the negative chatter that replays over and over in your mind?

Call to Action:

1) To start a new habit, you must first notice when you are repeating an old habit that doesn't work. Start observing yourself. Notice when you are asking yourself disempowering questions.

2) Take ten minutes now and reframe all those things you are worried about and turn them into questions for possibility.

Example: From: "What if I fail?" to "What if I accomplish my goal more quickly and easily than I thought possible?"

Key Success Principle #3

Understand Your Reason "Why"

Having goals is great but it is also important to have a bigger vision. That vision encompasses the reason why achieving those goals is so important to you. Although money is compelling in and of itself, it is generally not a big enough reason for keeping most people committed and on course.

Your reason "why" needs to be a strong motivator for you to go past all the obstacles and reach your goal. For some people, it is purely self-motivated; for example, *'To create multiple streams of income so I can work fewer hours and have more time for my family and friends.'*

The reason "why" can also take the form of a purpose statement. A purpose statement is generally self-motivated and also is about contributing to the welfare of others. For example, *My purpose is to empower people to live out their dreams with ease and abundance.* I am passionate about this for myself and for others. I have learned that the things we are most passionate about changing in our own lives are often what we are passionate about providing to others. I see this time and time again when I work with my clients to identify their purpose.

How John Got Grounded in His Reason Why:

John had a strong reason "why" that propelled him to succeed in real estate. He did it because he believed it would give him more time, which would allow him to mend his marriage and stay with his family. At the time, he was in a lot of pain and at risk of losing his family. Pain is often a strong motivator and leads to the reason "why." But the reason "why" does not have to arise from pain. It can also come from passion.

We all need a strong reason "why" to motivate us to make big changes in our lives. Without that, we are likely to keep falling back into old habits.

Coaching Questions:

1) What is the "why" behind your goal or vision?

2) Is it big enough to keep you motivated?

Call to Action:

1) Write down your "why" and post it in three visible places where you will see it every day.

2) Create a purpose statement that describes what you are passionate about providing in the world.

If you need help with this, consider ordering the workbook, Is Your Ladder Leaning Against the Wrong Wall?, *listed in the Resource section.*

My Purpose is:

My Key Learnings from This Chapter:

1)

2)

3)

Chapter #7:
Lisa Earle McLeod

Humorist and Author of *Forget Perfect*

*Leaves Fortune 100 Company and Pursues
Her Passion to Help Other Women*

Chapter 7

. . . .

Lisa Earle McLeod
Speaker, Humorist and Author of *Forget Perfect*

"Insist on yourself; never imitate. Your own gift you can present every moment with the cumulative force of a whole life's cultivation; but of the adopted talent of another you have only an extemporaneous half possession... Do that which is assigned to you, and you cannot hope too much or dare too much."
- Ralph Waldo Emerson

I'm here today with Lisa McLeod, who is a speaker and author of the book, *Forget Perfect*. She's also a wife and a mother of two young children.

Lisa, tell us what you did before you were a speaker and an author.

Back when I had a real job—one of those 'show-up-everyday, pantyhose' kind of jobs—I actually was in sales. My first job out of college was as a salesperson for a big consumer products company, Proctor and Gamble. I was with them for about five years, and then I was in the sales-training business for a number of years. That's how I made the leap to being a speaker and an author; I was in sales and marketing training and I had a couple of pivotal moments.

One time I was out to dinner with a number of women after I'd done a day-long training program with them. They were talking about what they worried about in their personal lives. I just remember thinking, "Tomorrow, instead of helping them identify their top 25 prospects, I'd really like to continue *this* conversation and talk more about what else is going on their lives." That's when I knew I needed to be doing something different.

You were more interested in helping these women in a whole different way than by helping them sell these products.

Exactly.

How successful were you as a salesperson?

I think I was a really good salesperson. I did pretty well at Proctor and Gamble. I say pretty well, because it was obvious to me at the time, and it's more obvious now, that I was never going to break through the ranks of middle management, for a whole host of reasons. The biggest one was, I wasn't a fit with the company. It took me a long time to realize that because I'd been thinking, "Other people are getting promoted ahead of me; I either don't have the right boss, I don't have the right person promoting me, or I've done some things wrong. I need to change, and I need to be different." It took me a long time to realize: I don't fit here, and that's not a bad thing.

I think what you went through is a very common experience for people. First, they initially blame things on their boss: "It's my boss' fault; he doesn't see how great I am."

And then they might start thinking, "Gosh, I've had three different bosses and none of them see how great I am so whoo whoo! Maybe it's me!

It was a real conflict for me because I had a lot of self confidence and thought I was great at what I was doing but still I was thinking: Why is it not happening? It took me a long time to realize it was because I wasn't that great at it. And I think that's one of the problems that I experienced and what a lot of people experience. I think if you are reasonably smart and you are hard working, you will be good at it. And because people are saying to you, "Oh, you're so good at this, you're this, this, this," you are achieving some certain level of success. But it's never going to be what you want until you find what you are *great* at.

Weren't you also thinking that you should feel lucky to have a position like you had and others would die for the position you were in?

Yes, that reminds me of the reaction I got from people who were close to me.

I had got a job with P&G right out of school, a coveted sales job with P&G. It never even dawned on me to think about whether or not I wanted it, because when they came after you and recruited you and you got the job–it was just everything! I remember I was thinking about leaving P&G and I was trying to decide what I was going to do. I had not gotten a promotion, and so that sort of got me thinking about looking at other jobs and other companies. I interviewed with Nabisco, Pepsi, and Coke and I got offered jobs that were at a level that was one up from where I was with a little bit more money. It took going through that process to realize that they're all basically the same, and that I didn't like that business.

I started looking for something else, because I didn't think I was going to get promoted. And then I did get promoted, but I had already had that aha! moment where I realized, I don't really like this industry, and I don't really like big business. Then I interviewed at this training company, that was smaller than Proctor and Gamble, which had billions of dollars in sales and millions of employees. This new company was a six million dollar company, and it had about 30 employees. The guy that was interviewing me was an ex-P&G person, and he was interviewing me for a sales rep. job, and I had been a manager of managers. I'd had lots of people working for me. I remember saying, well, how can I work my way up into management of this thirty-person company? I realized that the only way would be to have *his* job.

He said to me, "Well, do you really want to manage a bunch of people or do you just want to make more money?" I remember thinking about it–that actually I didn't want to manage people; I'm a terrible manager.

So, to get back to your point about people might be saying, how can I quit, I'm so lucky to have this job–the thought of selling these training programs was hugely appealing to me. I would be calling on big companies and selling them a program for making their communication skills excellent, and a whole host of other things. This was something I really thought would have a significant impact on the company and the people. I told my father and my husband about it, "I think I'm going to leave P&G and I'm going to take this job." They said, "I cannot believe you would give this up when you've just been promoted and Proctor and Gamble has been so good to you." My dad happened to be visiting at the time and finally, I remember sitting them both down and saying, "Here's the deal. I wake up every day and I hate to go to work. Is that what you want for me for the rest of my life? I hate it. I don't like my job. Is that what you think I deserve?" They both looked at each other and said, "Well, I guess when you put it that way…"

It took a lot of courage to say that to them.

It took me a long time to realize it myself. I should say, P&G is a great company. I had lots of friends do really well there–rise up in the ranks of senior management, love their jobs. I met some great people there and I'm still friends with them today. But it just wasn't for me.

There are lots of jobs out there and all of them are a good fit for someone.

For someone.

But none of them are a good fit for everyone.

I had in my mind what the really good jobs are. And I thought the really smart person–if they're not going to be a doctor or a scientist, for instance–the really smart businessperson ought to be able to go and work for a big company and work their way to the top. That was my benchmark of success. I think one's first reaction can be that it's the company; something's wrong with them. Or something's wrong with the people you're working with, and then your next reaction might be, "Oh, gosh, maybe I'm not as smart as I thought I was!" But it really is a matter of stepping back and saying, "Maybe this just isn't the thing for me."

What did you discover is the thing for Lisa and that makes Lisa great? Where are your natural talents?

I really enjoyed working for that training company. I did really well there and ended up going on and doing seminars myself, and I really liked that. But one of the things that I was always known for was being the funny girlfriend who can make you feel better about your life. If you ever have a problem, call up Lisa and she'll chat you up, tell you a bunch of funny stories, and then, at the end, you'll feel better about your life.

So the other thing I used to do was write these Christmas letters. And you know how you get those Christmas letters that say, "Joe just got promoted to King of the Universe, and Susie just solved World Hunger, and you know, me, I just got the Martha Stewart Award for domestic bliss." Well, I would write a Christmas letter that told the reality of our life, such as this is the year my kids got head lice, you know, those kinds of things. They were really funny letters, and a lot of people would respond, "I can't wait to get your letter, it's so funny." I think ignorance was bliss, in this case. I had never written anything besides business proposals, but I got the idea I was going to write a book and be the funny girlfriend who makes you feel better about your life.

I talked to a lot of women about what's wrong about their lives and what they'd like to do differently and that was where I came up with the premise for my first book, which was, *Forget Perfect*. Everybody's got this perfect little picture of how their lives should be and it keeps them from enjoying the way things are. So I had a little bit of doubt; I'm not a shrink, I'm not this renowned expert. But that's when I came back to just being the funny girlfriend. That's who you are, and I think one of the reasons why I first doubted it is because when something's really easy for you, you assume it's easy for everybody and it's not an important skill. What I realized through the course of writing some of the manuscript and having everybody read it is that everybody *can't* do that. Just because it's easy for you doesn't mean that people aren't willing to pay for it.

Yes, I see this frequently with my clients. People often think that because they do some things well and easily, it's easy for everyone. But this is not true, as in your case, not everyone is the funny girlfriend.

You think: That's no big deal, everybody can do that, and it's nothing. And you miss that it's your true calling–the stuff that's easy for you but not for everybody.

You said, ignorance is bliss and that you just decided to write this book. But the fact is, you were doing something that came easily to you; you were being who you truly are and were putting it down on paper.

I wasn't trying to do anything else. I'm really glad I didn't talk to other writers before I wrote the book, because I thought, well, you write this book, you send it to Random House, and they show up at your door with a briefcase full of money. Isn't that the way it works? The next thing you know, there you are on Oprah. And it didn't work exactly that way, but it did work surprisingly easily for me. I sent the book out to agents, I got some feedback from one of them–you probably want to change this and this. She sold it to Penguin Putnam and that whole process took about a year. I've since come to find out that the fact that getting a book published when I had no credentials, had never written anything, and didn't really have a platform from which to launch the book–that was a big deal. But, again, I didn't talk to anybody beforehand.

Isn't it a blessing that you didn't?

I'm so glad that I didn't because if I'd talked to anybody, they would have said, "Oh, you need to write for magazines first; you need to do this, you need to do that." But I was really writing what I believed in and it was very genuine. Now, I will say that I did write a big marketing plan because, of course, I had a background in sales and marketing. I was able to present it fairly well to the publisher. But to make a long story short, that part went very well for me. The part that did not go as smoothly, and took me by complete surprise, was how hard it was to promote it.

Before we talk about promotions, I remember you mentioning to me that you took a class on how to write a book.

I did, I took a class. I had written about half of the manuscript and was completely ignorant. I wondered how does one go about getting a publisher? The whole time I'm writing, I'm assuming that I'm going to get one, and so I took this class, a little two-night class, and the guy that taught the class is this 85-year-old guy. He's funny as all get out, and he comes in and he reads this quote, "There are many wonderful writers that will never achieve commercial success, simply because they lack the sales and marketing skills, and there are a number of other mediocre writers that, because they are such savvy marketers, will go on to great fame and fortune." The whole class is just crestfallen, they have their heads down, and my partner and I are in the back going, "That is us!" We are doing the dance of joy, because we're thinking, you know, mediocre writers, great marketers, that's us!

And we did end up having to come up with a decent book in the end. But the other thing that he said that got everybody really depressed was, "The odds of anybody in this class getting published are 1,000 to 1." And I thought, that is great because I'm looking around, and there were 20 of us in there. I thought, all I need to do is find another 980 and that's the 1,000 because I'm the one.

Most people would respond to that thinking, "I'll never be that one; the odds are so bad, how could I possibly?" And you said, "I can be that one."

I *will* be the one. One reason it was easier to respond that way is because the second he said it; I saw 20 heads go down. I thought, "Well, that's 20 of them right there that it's not going to happen for." So you figure, this guy teaches this class probably several times a year over a period of years, so that's half the thousand that aren't getting published right there.

Some math wizards will question your math but that's not what is relevant here. The two important points I'm hearing are: One, your belief that you could do it; you could be that one in 1,000 and you just went for it. Number two is that you had already tapped into, "This is what I'm good at, I'm the funny woman," and "This is what I'm passionate about–I want to help women." You were being yourself, you were using your natural talents, and you believed you could do it.

Right, it was that and we all hear so often about the power of positive thinking. Believe in yourself. It seems so hokey sometimes. And when you're doing what you were meant to do, nobody has to tell you that, it comes right from you and you know it. The second you start doing it, it's like a key turning in the lock. You say, "I'm really good at this." A lot of times we don't recognize what a big deal that is, but you feel it. It's those moments when you lose all track of time. There are moments when it's easy, when you're laughing, when you're having fun–that's when you know that this is what you were meant to be doing.

I certainly had people tell me at Proctor and Gamble, "Believe in yourself, you can do it." That helps to a certain extent, but that's only going to last so long. It has to come from you. Other people can certainly boast for you, and I had a number of people tell me, "This is really good, you need to be doing this, this is what you need to be doing," but at some point, it does have to come from you.

I remember I had a friend that took one of my early chapters to her book club. It was a writing group that met every week at a local bookstore. They all wrote things and passed them around, and she took one of my early chapters. I had used all kind of slang in my writing; language such as, "Get over yourself, honey." This one woman, an ex-English teacher, was so critical; she just ripped it to shreds. She had been published before, and even took the time to write up a little letter for me about why it was so very bad. This is before I'd gotten any interest from publishers; I remember getting that letter and thinking, "Oh my gosh, maybe I was wrong." Then I thought, you know, she might be accurate in everything she says, but guess what? This letter's boring to read, it's not funny, and it makes me feel worse about myself, so that's the exact opposite of what I'm trying to do. I'm trying to be interesting and funny, and make you feel better about yourself. So if this woman doesn't like it, she's probably right, it's not for her because she's in a totally different frame of mind than I'm in.

What a healthy place for you to come from.

I had help. That was a really hard thing to do. Reading that letter wasn't completely devastating but it did hurt. I remember showing the letter to my husband and he said, "God, sounds like a cranky old bitch." That kind of changed it for me. I thought, he's right; this person is just coming from a different place. You just have to let that kind of criticism slide off your back.

From our previous conversations I am also under the impression that while you were trying to write the book, you didn't tell a lot of people what you were doing. You didn't expose yourself to the possibility of people trying to discourage you.

That wasn't intentional, but it was a good thing that I didn't talk to people because it seems as if you share it, it loses its power. I remember almost feeling like I had a little surprise, a little secret I was nurturing along, and I remember being in exercise class one day and looking around at all the other people and thinking, these people have no idea that I have this hysterically funny, insightful, brilliant book inside me. And I'm writing it right now and they have no idea. But keeping it to myself seemed to make it stronger.

You built yourself up and didn't expose yourself to what others might think. There seemed to be a great deal of motivation coming from inside of you. When there was negative feedback about what you were doing, you were able to be objective and say, "That's just one person's opinion." As opposed to "It's the end of the world."

But an agent did reject me early on, who gave me some critical feedback. She said, it's not organized enough, it's not this, and it's not this. And she was right.

That was very different critical feedback, however. It wasn't just, "You're an idiot," it was, "You have a good idea, you present it well, but you need to do a few specific things." I called her on the phone and said, "You've obviously thought about this. Could you give me a little more information?" She talked me through it so that I could say, "It sounds as if I need to do this, this, and this—which was basically to organize the book differently and better." She said, "That's exactly what you need to do. If you do that, send it back to me." And she is my agent now.

The difference was that you really looked at each piece of feedback that you got and said, "What's the value of this? What are they saying, and is it something I need to take to heart?"

Should this person just be completely ignored, or do I need to pay attention to them? And it's really hard to do. You have to develop a tough skin to do that, but I think–especially when it's something that's very personal such as your writing, your art, your decorating, or your music–that people are going to have a lot of differences of opinion. It's hard to distinguish the difference between those times when it's just not for them, and those times when you assess that the person knows what they're talking about so you can accept; I do need to change this.

It seems to be a matter of evaluating the advice you're getting, who it's coming from, and what they're saying. And listening to yourself so that you ask yourself, "Does this make sense for what I'm doing, does this ring true?"

The matter of your response to authority figures into this as well. I have a friend who makes beautiful greeting cards, hand-made greeting cards. They're absolutely wonderful and she made them all her life. When she was in an art show as a senior in college, this one well-known commercial artist in the card business looked at her work and said, "You're creating stuff for a world that doesn't exist. Nobody is going to buy this." She let that piece of feedback haunt her for years and years. And he was right; she was creating stuff for a world that didn't exist. But that world needed to exist. He was saying, "You're creating these $6 and $7 cards; no one is going to buy these, because there is no platform in the market for people to buy those."

But the reality was that there were a lot of women out there who really loved the idea of giving a card as the gift itself. There were people who loved buying these amazing cards and sending them to their friends. There was a whole market that wasn't even recognized at that time. And she said, "I don't even know this person, this man who said this to me. Those words rang in my ears for 10 miserable years in corporate America, until I finally thought, I will die if I do not go make these cards." It's amazing that we let someone do that to us, especially when they are the perceived authority figure. Sometimes the authority figure knows what they're talking about, but not always. If you've got a secret fear inside yourself, their critical words will ring true to you, but it doesn't mean they're correct. They may be only projecting their own fears.

It takes some strength to look at it objectively.

It does, as well as to get people supporting you. Apparently, unbeknownst to me, my family had this little powwow, behind my back, where they discussed my project. My father, my brother, my sister and even my husband had a conversation to discuss, "Does Lisa really have a prayer of getting a book published?" My dad actually knew something about the publishing business. But even though they didn't think I knew what I was doing, and I probably wouldn't be able to get it published, they decided that they wouldn't say anything, and they were just going to support me. They said, "That sounds great, Lisa; go ahead!" I did not even know that until after I got the deal with Putnam that they had done that. The book came out and I did this big event near where my parents live, and the whole town came out for it. I gave this talk and signed books and my dad said, "You know, I have to tell you, we really wondered about this."

What a gift that they didn't rain on your parade.

They didn't rain on my parade, *and* it never even showed. Because I think even though they were thinking that I had a million to one chance, a little part of each of them still thought, "Well, the odds are really bad, but maybe she'll do it. The last thing we want to do is tell her no when she hasn't even tried, so let's just support her and then if it doesn't work out, we'll be supportive of that, too."

You mentioned that promoting the book didn't flow quite as easily for you as publishing it.

Well, it had been out a week and Oprah had not called, and I just could not believe it. Well, where was she? The title of the book is *Forget Perfect: Finding Joy, Meaning and Satisfaction In The Life You've Already Got, and the You You Already Are.* It's all about being, making a difference, connecting with other people, being a better friend, and discovering the best of who you already are. If I had a dollar for every person that has come up to me and said, "Have you tried to get your book on Oprah? Have you thought of that?" I would be a very rich woman.

But it is really hard to crack the media. Now I've been on television shows all over the country; I've been on radio shows all across the country. But registering on the general public's radar screen is a very hard thing to do. The first week the book came out, I went into a bookstore in Atlanta where I live, and it was a big, huge bookstore, and there was my book, several copies, on the front table of new releases. I thought, "I've arrived, I'm here, there it is, my book, my words right there." I'm all excited, and then I meet the manager. I say, I'm an author, this is my book, and he asked, "Oh, will you sign your copies?" It's great, I signed all my copies.

Then I go down the street to another big chain bookstore, and I look for my book. I can't find it. So I find the management, and they say, "Oh, we haven't put out the books that were released this week. Let's go in the back and see if we can find it so you can sign your copies." We go in the back, and there is this giant wall of all the books that have been released this week. It was so humbling because I just remember looking at them and thinking, oh my gosh, why would I ever think that anyone would pay attention to my one little book.

I had to spend the better part of the whole next year trying to get media interviews and get quoted in magazines. One of the things I realized is that even though a lot has happened, and it worked, and it has registered on the public's radar screen, it's really a weird spot to be in. You're totally self-absorbed, so I write this book about how to find joy and meaning in life, about making a difference and connecting to other people, and I spend the better part of a year completely self-absorbed. I realized that there was not going to be any long-term satisfaction in that.

Perhaps it's a good time for us to look at what's next for Lisa. What do you want to create next for yourself?

What I did really did work, so it's hard to look back on that year and realize I lost my sense of what was really important to me. I'm now working on a second book. I just got a column with Lifetime Magazine, and it's called "Forget Perfect." That's exciting for me. The first book was about Forget Perfect for yourself; the second one is about how to let everyone else off the hook as well. I'm working on that now and trying to get myself more centered on doing a better job with other people–listening to them and paying attention to them.

How do you define success?

It's really a twofold thing to me. I know that a lot of people talk about balanced living, about finding balance in your life. That's a struggle right now because for me, success has a couple of components. One is a level of influence over people, and it's not so much to sell this many copies and be on Oprah, although that would certainly be nice. I've really tried to get myself back to focusing on what I want to do to have a positive impact on women.

The hard part of it is balancing that with caring for my two small children. I think a lot of women today are discovering what men always knew: Work is easier. I could give a speech, everybody claps, they laugh, they cry, they think about the meaning of life, they come up, they buy a book, they tell me how much I help them, and that is really a neat experience. You're never going to have that same kind of experience with your family. So it's easy to turn away from your family and go for what feels like more success to you. But at the end of the day, my personal relationships are how I define success.

And, yet, that's a hard thing. I could spend 45 minutes talking to my kids and there's never going to be a moment where they'll say, "Oh mom, boy, I discovered the meaning of life through talking to you."

How else could people know that their personal relationships are a success other than being told that you've had an impact on their lives?

That's why the next book is *Forget Perfect For Them*. Because I think we all tend to believe that the perfect husband, the perfect kids, the perfect boss would spend all their time telling you how much you've changed their lives. Well, those people exist in sitcoms and sappy novels. We need to recognize there is no way that you're going to experience the same level of unqualified bliss with your family with everyday interpersonal relationships that you might experience in short-term stints out in the workplace. With people that you live and work with every day, there are going to be highs, there are going to be lows, there are good times, and bad times, and what you're really looking for is an overall feeling. As a mom, a lot of times you can feel as if a lot of it is negative. You're so behind on everything, you're trying to keep up with it, you have to be the disciplinarian, and you're catching yourself screaming at your kids. You're constantly thinking, oh my gosh, we're going to be late...why aren't you kids eating your vegetables? And so on. It doesn't feel like success to you. I think you just really have to change your way of thinking. What you're really going for is at the end of the day, you can raise adults that go out and function in society; then you did it. Jackie Kennedy once said, "If you mess up with your kids, nothing else you do really matters very much." And that is really true.

It appears to be about influence.

It's about influencing others.

You influence women in one way and you get one kind of feedback. You influence your children in another way, and get a whole different kind of feedback.

Well, the thing is, when you write something or speak, people will sometimes tell you, "You really changed my life," or, "You changed the way I thought about this and it had a major impact on me." But there is absolutely no way in a book or a speech that you can have the kind of impact on them that the people they're with every day have on them.

Do you advocate having a goal or purpose rather than focusing on feedback from others?

If you have a goal such as wanting to reach a million women, then if you don't get on Oprah, it doesn't feel like failure. There are a lot of vehicles with which you can go down that path. If my goal with my children is to raise functioning adults and my goal with my husband is that he consistently considers me to be a supportive person, then my focus is on them.

As a woman, you get out there and get a publicist, an agent, people prepping you for your speeches, and so on. And it seems to become all about you. They're all supporting you. Now, some of that's their job and that's what they're good at. But it's really hard to step back and return to your regular life and play that role for somebody else. You've gotten so accustomed to saying, "Well, it's time for me to go on. Do you have my water out there?" and you know, "Are you guys all set up with the books so all I have to do is sit here and look good and sign them?" "OK, perfect, we're all set."

But, no one's doing that for you at home. You could get a million maids and nannies, but emotionally, if you want to support your children and you want to support your spouse, you're the one that has to do it.

To sum up what I'm hearing, it's about focusing on what is it you want to provide versus focusing on what you're going to get back.

Yes, and I have noticed that in both my inner world of my family and my outer world, the more I focus on what I really want these people to feel, think, believe as a result of interacting with me, the better things go for me. Even just in general: I write better, I speak better, and I'm so much better with my family when I think,

"How do I want them to feel as a result of interacting with me?" One of the little tests that I have used with my kids that really works in my own mind, is imagining that I am raising the President which, of course, in my case is true, I am…

Of course!

We're imagining we're here in the year 2035, and I am raising the President, the person that's one day going to have their finger on the button. What will I wish I'd done in this situation or that one? Sometimes it may have been to cut them more slack, sometimes it's to be harder on them, sometimes it's to teach them more about tolerance, and sometimes it's to teach them about following the rules. It's different every time. But this person is going to be making these major decisions. What will I wish I had taught them, and it helps me make better decisions when I'm with them to play that game in my mind.

Lisa, there's a lot of wisdom here and women will be able to relate to being a mother and being a businesswoman and balancing all of it. Thank you for being so honest and sharing yourself with us. What is the Web site where people can learn more about your book?

ForgetPerfect.com. It includes a funny quiz, "Are you trying to be too perfect?"

Great. Thank you so much, Lisa.

Thanks.

Three Key Success Principles Plus Coaching Questions and Action Steps

• •

Lisa Earle McLeod

Key Success Principle #1:

Streamline Your Efforts: Align Your Natural Talents with Your Goal

Success comes easier and more quickly when you enhance your strengths and delegate in areas where you are weak. If you think you must conquer the things you are not good at and prove you can do them, you are in for a long, hard journey. It is also is a good idea to delegate those things you can do but don't enjoy doing. For example, I am good at paperwork and research but don't enjoy doing them. When I delegate these tasks, I enjoy my work much more and get more done.

Your natural talents are those things you do so easily and naturally that you think they are no big deal. Many of my clients were overlooking their natural talents when they first came to me. They thought if it is this easy for them, it must be this easy for everyone. This is rarely the case.

The key is to take your natural talents and abilities and strengthen them through education and experience. You are not born an expert at anything. It is something you develop.

How Lisa Aligned with Her Natural Talents:

For a while, Lisa could not understand why her bosses couldn't recognize how great she was. Then she realized that while she is great, she wasn't great at this job, nor did she really fit in at Proctor & Gamble.

Lisa's innate talent is to be the funny girlfriend who can make you feel good about yourself. At first, she rejected this because it was something she did so easily she thought anyone could do it. The fact is, not anyone can do it like she does. When she started being the funny girlfriend in her book and on the speaking platform, she felt fulfilled and her career began to take off.

Coaching Questions:

1) Are you fully utilizing your gifts in your current career?

2) What would you like to be doing more of?

Call to Action:

1) If you are uncertain as to what your natural talents and abilities are, you can interview your friends and co-workers and get their insights. You may be surprised to learn how others see you. To obtain a free interview form, go to the Resources Section.

2) If you would like an objective opinion about your natural talents, take the Rockport Career Test. This is the best assessment I have found to truly assess your natural talents and abilities. It is a timed test that you can take in your own home. It gives you objective feedback rather than asking you what you think you are good at. For more information on the test, go to the Resources Section.

3) If you know what your natural gifts are, list the ways you could more effectively use them in your career.

4) List the tasks you are doing currently that do not fit with your natural gifts or desires and find people to delegate them to. If you do not have any employees, consider hiring freelance help or bartering.

Key Success Principle #2

Say "Nay" to the Judges in Your Life: Do What You Love

One of the biggest things that keeps people in careers in which they are unhappy is the thought that "they should be happy." Time and time again I see people in prestigious jobs who are making a good living, but feel empty, unfulfilled, or like they have to keep up a facade.

The interviews in this book describe different people who are happy and successful in a variety of different careers. Just because it is a great career for them, does not mean it will be a great career for you. The purpose of these stories is to show you the philosophies and actions that made these people successful when they were doing something they loved.

A great career match needs to have several components:

1) Something you are passionate about
2) A match for your natural talents
3) A work environment that is conducive to your personality

If any of these components is not a match, then it is likely that the job is not the best one for you.

How Lisa Left a Career that Was Not a Fit for Her:

Lisa's family and friends thought she had the greatest job in the world and she would be crazy to give it up. They meant well; they only wanted the best for Lisa but they didn't know that deep inside herself, Lisa was truly unhappy.

Lisa realized she didn't like big business and also got in touch with her passion when she noticed she would rather be helping her female clients with their personal situations than helping them sell a product.

Upon realizing these things for herself, she eventually found the courage to tell her father and husband that she was miserable in the career that everyone thought was so great for her.

Coaching Questions:

1) Do you make decisions based on what others think is good for you or what you *know* is right for you?

2) Who is running your life?

3) Do you fit in your current career and work environment or are you trying to make yourself fit?

If you are unsure about your answer, notice whether you feel free to be yourself or if you are constantly working at being how you think you need to be.

4) Is there something you would rather be doing than what you are doing now? If so, what is it?

5) If you like what you are doing, notice if there is anything holding you back from doing it *in the way* you really want to? If so, what is it?

Call to Action:

1) If you are questioning whether your career is the best fit for you, allow yourself to be in an inquiry of what careers or environments would be a better fit.

If you feel stuck, consider hiring a career coach to help you discover your right livelihood and move past the obstacles so you can make it happen.

2) If you know what you would prefer to be doing, make a commitment right now to find a way to make that dream a reality. Get support from a coach, friend or mentor to move through your fears and blocks.

3) If you are in the right career for you, make a commitment to do it in the way that works best for you. If it works best for you, it will work out for the best for others as well.

Key Success Principle #3

What's the Locus of Your Focus?

Get Out Of Your Head and Focus on Your Customers' Needs

Most of the world is egocentric. We tend to think everything is about us. But really, none of this is about you or me. It is not about how great you are or could be. And it's not about what others think of you.

Success comes when you focus on what you are providing to others. When you focus over there—on what you are offering to other people—you are connected to whatever you are doing. As a result, things will tend to flow. Conversely, when you are focused on yourself and how you are performing, you are "in your head." In these situations you may find yourself stumbling over your own words, making silly mistakes, forgetting what you were going to say, etc.

It is impossible to be connected to others while you are in your head. When you are passionate about what you are providing and keep that purpose in the forefront of what you do, you naturally perform better. In addition, people sense your authenticity and are drawn to you as a result.

How Lisa Focuses on What She Is Providing To Others:

Lisa connects success with being able to influence others in a positive way. She wants to have a positive impact on women across the globe and with her spouse and children. She gets different feedback from each of these groups and has come to realize the amount of feedback does not necessarily equal the amount of influence. She has learned that she gets better results when she focuses on what she is going to provide versus what she is going to get.

Coaching Question:

1) Where/when do you focus on what you are providing and where/when do you focus on what you are going to get?

Notice how you feel when you do each.

Call to Action:

1) I challenge you to spend the entire day focusing on what you are providing to others and see what happens.

Do you accept that challenge?

My Key Learnings from This Chapter:

1)

2)

3)

Chapter #8:

The Psychology of Living Out Your Dreams

Special Value-Added Section

Dr. Van K. Tharp,
Psychologist and Trading Coach

*How to Recognize Common
Self-Sabotaging Behaviors and
Move Through Them*

Chapter 8

. . . .

The Psychology of Living Out Your Dreams

with Dr. Van K. Tharp

"I seldom think about my limitations, and they never make me sad. Perhaps there is just a touch of yearning at times; but it is vague, like a breeze among flowers."

- Helen Adams Keller

I am here today with Dr. Van Tharp. Van is a psychologist and professional trading coach, and founder of the International Institute of Trading Mastery.

ᎶᏉ

We'll be talking about the psychology of living out your dreams and the psychology of trading, and what we as human beings do to get in the way of making all those good things happen for ourselves.

But first, how did you get involved in this field? That's an unusual occupation.

Well, I was trading in graduate school, and I had about $20,000 accumulated, and I lost it all. Then about five years later I did it all

230

again; I lost it all. About 90% of the trades went against me, so I decided it couldn't be chance, it must be me. As a researcher, which is my background, I decided to figure out what was wrong with me, and as I started doing the research, I found out there were a lot of other people in the same boat. That evolved into a coaching system.

At the time you lost your first $20,000, were you in graduate school for psychology?

Yes. My background in graduate school has nothing to do with what I do for a living. I mean, there are certainly areas of decision-making now that are related to what I do, but my area was biological psychology. I'm trained as a researcher.

Your interest was purely a matter of your own circumstances in life and investigating how to change that?

And discovering everybody else made the same mistakes that I did. I started doing research, people wanted help, and I didn't know what to do to help them. I then started trying to figure out what to do to help them, and the whole business evolved out of that.

Basically, you saw a problem and decided to figure out how to solve it. What did you see about yourself, in terms of why you kept losing that money? What did you notice about yourself that's also prevalent in other people?

I think it was happenstance at the time. I was trading options, and most people lose trading options. In fact, they lose 90% of the time. I was just too naïve to know that. So I made the assumption that it was me. And in one sense, that assumption was correct. It was me. It always is the person doing the trading.

Would it be fair to say it was a combination of not knowing enough about options or a system for options, along with you and your thought process?

Well, I would say probably a hundred different things at this point. There are many things that I didn't know at the time that would have made an incredible difference. As we get into this, we can talk about that.

To clarify, you help people become better traders and investors. You do that both by teaching them how to create a system that works for them and by looking at what they do that gets in the way.

Right. I consider myself as having two primary functions. First, I'm a modeler. That means I find people who do things well, and you've got to have a number of them. I determine what they do in common, and then for those commonalities, I determine the beliefs, strategies, and mental states that are necessary to duplicate that. If I get it right, I can teach it to others, and they can get it right, too.

And then, the second part is that I'm a trading coach. What a coach typically does is find very talented people, and that's what I found over the years, it tends to be talented people who are attracted to what I do, as opposed to, say, the average person. A talented person will tend to come in and say, "I need a coach; I want to get that extra edge." So I find talented people. Then I make sure that they're following the fundamentals of my modeling work. Then, if they're not, the problem is usually some form of self-sabotage. I help them with that.

You are probably one of a few people out there who focuses on the psychology or the self-sabotaging aspect of trading. How do people get in their own way with that? And, then expand on how people sabotage themselves and their dreams.

I have six things on my list. For the most part, these would apply to any area. It doesn't take much to generalize.

The first thing is, we're all creative beings. We create our lives. Most people give up that responsibility and become victims in many ways in their lives. Our society teaches us to do that. People will think that things happen *to* them. As an example, in the stock market, many people have lost a lot of money. So they look for someone to blame. They blame CEO's of companies. They blame their analysts. They blame their broker. They blame the bear market, all sorts of things. This simply signifies they can't figure out all the mistakes that they've made and correct them, and they'll probably repeat the same mistakes over and over again. That's what most people do; they assume somebody else is responsible for what happens to them. That means they can never correct mistakes.

They point the finger, rather than taking responsibility.

Absolutely. The next item on the list of ways people sabotage themselves comes a bit out of Robert Kiyosaki, to a certain extent. Kiyosaki, who wrote *Rich Dad, Poor Dad,* says people have different mentalities, in terms of what I call systems. Most people have an employee mentality, in which they work for somebody, and they learn a particular system. They don't even realize the system under which they're operating. They say, "Well, tell me what to do, and tell me what happens next." They want to be spoon-fed.

People in the market say, "Tell me what the market's going to do, tell me what's going to happen next." That's what happens with all the people on television that they listen to. Those TV experts just tell them what they think the market's going to do. It really has nothing to do with success, because what they're not doing is developing their own method, or something that fits them–a system that works for them. And, systems can be quite simple, but people who trade do need to follow a system.

People tend to rely on others for their success and want to be told what to do versus educating themselves and learning a system that works for them?

Yes. The third item on my list of ways people get in their own way is really obvious. It applies to every area you can think of. That is, that people need to be right. They need to believe that they're right about things. Think about it: We go through a whole school system, whether it's 12 years or 20 years, in which you're taught that the teacher is right, and if you don't get 70%, you're a failure. You've got to get at least 94% to get an excellent grade. And, teachers are basically saying, we can show you how you can do that. This has nothing to do with other areas of life.

As trading experts, we say we can show you how you can be right 20% of the time in the market and make a lot of money. And simply put, the way to do that is, when you're wrong, you just lose what you risk, and when you win, you win ten times what you risk. That works out to a nice gain when you're only right 20% of the time.

But, what happens when people need to be right, when they have a profit, for example, they've got to take that profit right now. They end up cutting their winning short. When they're behind, they don't want to take the losses. So the losses grow and grow and grow, and that's the opposite of what you need to do to be successful in the markets. You need to let your profits grow and cut your losses short. I think this need to be right may apply to almost everything. People have to be right, as opposed to going with the flow and being willing to admit mistakes.

By needing to be right, do you mean believing we are making the correct decision keeps us stuck with our original choice rather than making changes as we go along?

One way to put it is, we're bound by our beliefs. I like to think of all of our beliefs as the things we decide to adopt at points in our lives because we think they're useful. It's really our filter to reality. And there's almost always a more useful belief, and if you have an attitude that all your beliefs are useful, and there might be something *more* useful, then you can evolve. But if you think that you're right, and everything you believe right now is the gospel truth, then you're in trouble and you'll never change.

It's about willing to be flexible versus staying with a tried past.

Right. The fourth factor, and an area that pertains to trading in particular, is this: There are all kinds of judgmental shortcuts that we make. These shortcuts really limit us. Because we have to cope with lots of information, it's natural for us to want to create shortcuts, but they can typically cause us to self-sabotage. I've mentioned a couple of these shortcuts: One way is being conservative about profits and risky about our losses. Another one is needing to be right. There are something like 30 or 40 of these shortcuts that have been documented in the psychological literature.

In general, when you say shortcut, if we again apply that out on a broader scope, do you mean the tendency to want to get somewhere faster and not do the things that we need to do along the way?

Well, not exactly. What happens is that we have a tremendous amount of information that we need to process. Our conscious capacity is limited to something like seven chunks of information. So we have all these shortcuts that we've developed over time to allow us to consume all stimuli, to handle this great deal of information. For instance, one very strong tendency is to simply say, well, what we already know is right, and anything else is wrong, so we'll filter that out. But that will filter out about 90% of the information coming in. So if you have an opinion about the market, for example, that the market's going to go up, and you're overdue for a big market gain, then any evidence to the contrary, you'll filter out.

It's a shortcut based on what we already assume is true.

Correct. Now the fifth factor that has us self-sabotage applies to almost every area of success: People don't know what the fundamental things are that they need to do. It's really that simple. In trading, for example, they might approach it as if they were going to the stock market. They assume they just need to pick the right stocks and if they buy them and hold on forever, they're going to get rich. That's what they're taught, and it really has nothing to do with that.

There are huge cycles in the market. We're in one of them in 2003–where buy and hold is absolute suicide. And the fundamentals of trading–here is one of them–I'd advise that you need to know when to get out before you ever enter any kind of position; you need to be able to control a risk on that. That means, for instance, you need to, not lose more than 1% of your portfolio on any given idea. That keeps you in the game for a long time. Those are just a couple of the fundamentals, but there are many, many more, such as having a business plan.

It's important to learn the basics before you jump in there and haphazardly make guesses.

Right. It's really interesting; I've modeled four areas: The basics of trading, and what I call position sizing, and system development, and the wealth process. I find that with every one of them, the natural tendency is to do all the wrong things.

Any thoughts on why that might be?

I have one idea, and I may be writing a book on this in a couple of years. The premise is that we all play a lot of games, and the games have hierarchies. Those people at the higher hierarchies tend to win the games and they make the rules. Most people just accept the rules at the higher hierarchies and act unconsciously. They don't even know there's an option of making up the rules.

Take, for example, the mutual fund. In the trading hierarchy, mutual funds make all their money by having your money with them. They get a percentage of their assets every year as a fee, and it doesn't matter whether they make money or not, they still get paid. So, naturally, it's to their advantage to tell everybody that you should buy stocks and hold them forever.

We're being told some things and we're moving around somewhat blindly, like cows in a herd.

The movie *The Matrix* is a good example. Everybody's asleep and they don't know it.

The last factor, the sixth one, is that we're full of self-sabotage because even when we know all of the stuff that I've just mentioned, most people won't apply it. I have lots of theories about self-sabotage, and we could probably talk about that forever, but I think the basic reason is that we're afraid to experience our own experiences. When we don't want to have an experience, we tend to suppress it. That totally suppresses our creative ability.

Can you give an example?

Well, I'll explain it in reference to our feelings. We have a lot of feelings. When we grow up, we're taught to label them in a way. Some feelings are good and it's OK to feel those, and then some feelings are bad, and it's not OK to feel those. For example, it's not OK to be angry and have a temper tantrum. Mom and Dad won't like that. It's not OK to be fearful. We're all taught, but especially little boys are taught, don't have fear. At least, I grew up with that John Wayne model: Don't experience your emotions. I think little girls get the same sort of thing to some degree also. When a negative emotion comes up we don't want to feel it. What typically tends to happen is you end up storing it in your body. That feeling wants to come up lots and lots, so it comes up in almost any situation, and until you're willing to really feel that feeling and get it out of your system, it's there. It keeps coming up and finding reasons to express itself. We work with this as an exercise with our clients.

Is it that we don't want to feel fear but since we're focused on not wanting to feel it, we tend to feel it all the time?

Right. Here's a good example. Suppose you find someone of the opposite sex attractive, and you approach them. This is the first time you've ever done this and you say, "Hello, do you want to go for a date?" or something like that. If they've had a bad day and just kind of look at you and say, "Get lost," suddenly you feel rejected. You suppress it by saying, "I wouldn't have wanted to go out with them anyway." So now, instead of feeling all those feelings, you have some stored rejection. A week later you see somebody else you want to approach. You start to approach them, and then all that chatter comes up in your head, "Oh, what if they reject me again?" Then all the feelings come up. And now, you feel rejected before anything's even happened. And you might tend to approach them very defensively and say something like, "You wouldn't want to go out with me…" which probably would produce the result you expected in the first place. It just becomes a vicious circle.

We focus on something we don't want and we create more of it. Let's expand on that. What if someone has a big dream and they're afraid of failing at it?

They'll experience the fear of failure all the time. And find ways to justify that.

They'll just prove that what they thought was going to happen is going to happen?

Absolutely.

How do you help people get past their fear of failure?

First of all, when somebody comes in, there's usually a hierarchy of things going on. I have to go to the bottom of the hierarchy. It's sort of an art form, figuring out what's at the bottom of the hierarchy. If you try to fix the solutions at the top, which is maybe that they do not understand the fundamentals, you teach them the fundamentals. You teach them why something is not going to work the way they thought it might. If there's some level below that that's causing the sabotage, that's not going to work. You have to find the deepest level of the thing that's not working in their thinking and actions and fix that. There are all sorts of models. But let's say the fear is the deepest level of what's not working. You would need to feel the feelings until it "pops." I don't recommend that people do that on their own. But if you get the feelings out of your system, it typically will go away.

One would then let it be all right to have those feelings?

Right.

Part of it is accepting where you are, being OK with that?

Yes, part of it.

Can you give us an example of someone who's been unsuccessful, or has been getting in his or her own way in trading and has been self-sabotaging? What happened with them before working with you, and what was possible when they got past that?

I'll give you a couple of examples of people who come to me. And, as I said, these tend to be the more successful types of people. I'll tell you an example about one of my clients, and I'll sort of give you some of the things that were going on with him and the order.

As he grew up, he always noticed that he had this feeling of emptiness. And as a compensation for that somewhat, he had a cousin that was his best friend. They did all kinds of wild things together. They were daredevils, doing all kinds of crazy things together, and they were best buddies. This guy (my client) developed a huge real estate business, did all sorts of very exciting things, and became a multi-millionaire. Almost everything he did turned to gold.

Then, his friend drowned. He was fishing and I guess he got drunk. He fell in the water and drowned, and my client grieved terribly. He thought, "If only I'd been there, I could have stopped him, or maybe it should have been me." Coincidentally, at that same time, his real estate empire seemed to crash around him. The bank called in a loan, and he couldn't understand why they were doing that because there was plenty of cash flow. But once that was called in, it was like that started off another one and pretty soon, he was bankrupt. He did keep some money on the side, however, so he went into trading with that money. And then he had some big losses in that trading. After that, he came to me, because he couldn't seem to make a go of it in the trading, and I noticed that he didn't have any understanding of the fundamentals as we teach them.

Now, let's go backwards in examining this to try to figure out what happened. When I would teach him some of the fundamentals, that didn't work. When I dealt with the big losses in trading, that wouldn't work. When I dealt with his real estate empire crashing, that didn't seem to work. But when I dealt with his friend drowning, it seemed to get some effects. Then when I dealt with the feelings of emptiness to begin with, that was the cause of it all. Fixing that one could build on all of the other circumstances. If you look at those layers of experiences, you can see that there's a hierarchy to it all.

You really have to get at the root because that's probably causing self-sabotage in other areas of your life, not just in one. People are not likely to think back to see, "Oh, when I was five, this is what happened," for instance.

Right, and it takes a lot of effort to get out that stuff. Most people are just thinking, "Well, why do I keep losing?"

Do you have any suggestions for how people might get at their own root cause, or do you suggest that they see a coach or a psychologist to do that?

I have a home study course. It's geared towards trading, but its exercises deal with stress, your beliefs, and a good bit else. About 20% of it is specific to trading, and the other 80% is general. It's five volumes and about 1,000 pages worth of exercises. That's what we recommend as a starting point, certainly for all investors and traders. I remember doing some coaching with a Japanese man once, and he didn't understand any English, so I had to take him through the whole course. His comment at the end was, "Gee, I thought this would help me in my trading, but I can apply it to my construction business just as well as anything else."

The key is really to get at the core, and mostly what we're dealing with is the symptoms and the outcomes, or the lack of outcomes.

What would you say, in general, if someone is not making any progress toward fulfilling a dream, and may be feeling stalled or stuck? What might be one thing that they could do?

They can look at a whole bunch of things that might be getting in the way. The first thing is to look at the extent to which they are committed to their dream. There's a theory about emotions that I call the Hamburger Theory. It will be fitting to tell this story.

Imagine you're traveling across country, you think you're going to Los Angeles, but you ended up someplace else. You're just traveling, and it's OK, and you go into this hamburger stand. You buy this hamburger, and it looks like the guy probably dropped the hamburger on the floor and it really tastes horrible. So you start to complain, and the guy argues with you and says, "These are the best hamburgers," and then you really start to get upset. You look and you see a lot of dirt and a cockroach on the floor. The next thing you know, you're getting everybody up in arms against this guy and his bad hamburgers. So you stop there for two weeks and you lead a whole crusade against this guy and his terrible hamburgers.

Now, contrast that with somebody who's got a real purpose in life. It's very important that they go across country and they know where they're going, they have an important meeting, they go in to the same hamburger store, they get the hamburger. They might not be very happy about it, but they simply throw the hamburger away and go to another store, get their hamburger, and then go off on their business. When people aren't committed to something, they find all sorts of things to sidetrack them. When they are committed, then everything seems to move to act in their favor.

You're saying we have the tendency to focus too much energy on the little things that don't really matter. And when you stay focused on whatever you want to achieve and let the other things glide off your back...

Yes, the way I like to think of it is that we all have a purpose in life, and if you find the purpose, then everything seems to work for you and you can become committed. Then things seem to fall in place. If things don't seem to fall in place, then you really haven't found your purpose. One good way of knowing is if it doesn't give you a lot of joy, then it's probably not your purpose.

It's a matter of what Joseph Campbell always said, "The purpose of your life is to follow your bliss."

I totally agree with the idea of finding your purpose and my experience is that you can find your purpose, but still be entrenched in old fears and things that get in the way of the purpose flowing.

Well, finding your purpose is the first layer. The second one is what we're brainwashed in; it's blaming others. When something goes wrong, we get into that thing of figuring out what happened to us, and we basically get into a victim mode, as opposed to a creation mode. With our legal system, you can think of almost anything and somehow trace it to being somebody else's fault, and you can find clear-cut evidence.

You can also find some example in there of how you could have prevented it, or how you actually caused it yourself. An example of this is when I first got into this kind of philosophy. I was driving my son to school and a car made a left-hand turn right in front of me. We had a head-on collision. I had some stitches and my car was totaled. Based on everything the law says, it was purely this guy's fault.

But, in attempting to live this philosophy, I thought to myself, I'm really going to stretch it. I'm going to figure out how I created this accident. As soon as I decided to look at that, it became very easy to figure it out: I had a 1975 Buick Skyhawk that was designed for a rotary engine, but GM decided not to make a rotary engine, and they put a V6 in it. That engine was too heavy for the front end, and it was always out of alignment. I was always going through tires, it always needed new brakes, and I had to do my own brake work. I replaced the brakes every 3,000 or 4,000 miles. I absolutely hated that car. I would have done anything to get rid of it. So, naturally, I was very receptive to having an accident with it, and of course, I got a new car out of it.

So what I'm hearing you say is that, and it's something that I believe fully, my thoughts will basically create my reality.

Absolutely.

Let's go back full circle. If you're thinking that you're not going to do well in the stock market, that's what's going to happen?

Let me give you an example of that, since this is something I know very well. In 1999, when people asked me what I did for a living and I said I was a trading coach, they'd ask me, "What's the market going to do, what stocks do you think I should buy?" And I said, "That's not what I do. I'd tell you to have a business plan. I think you should know exactly when you're going to get out of all of these stocks. You should have an exit plan. You should limit your risk to maybe 1%, 2% at most for every stock that you're in. I would show you how to do that," and they don't want to hear that. "Well, what's the market going to do?" And, most of them have lost 70% to 90% on their money. Some of them still have all their stocks, and now most of them are looking to file a lawsuit against some analyst, or they're blaming the executives of the company they held stock with because they were corrupt, or there were accounting errors. Or they want to sue their broker for recommending the stock in the first place.

So there are all kinds of things to figure out how they're not responsible for the mistake. If they start to look at the mistakes: a) they didn't have an exit plan; b) they didn't have any plan at all; c) they risked too much, and I could go on and on about what mistakes they made. As long as they're out there looking for someone to blame, that's the way it happens. I actually gave this talk at a conference recently. It was an options conference, and the audience was full of people who were drawn to the hype of making 500% on this trade, and 500% on that trade, 1,000% on this trade. This happens in days. I gave this kind of talk, and I found most of the people there would admit to making two or three of these mistakes. So I talked about how to correct these mistakes. What I found was that people totally turned off to that. They didn't want to hear about their mistakes. They said this psychology stuff is crazy; tell me how to make money.

Tell me how to do it, give me the quick fix answer; they wanted to blame somebody else. Why do you think people do this?

I think it's probably our cultural upbringing. Most of the professions in our society today have some aspect of dealing with how some people will cheat other people and we have got to protect you from that. We've got law enforcement, we've got the legal system, and we've got the medical system that says everything happens to you; all these germs invade your body, you don't have any control over the outcome. The accounting system says you can't keep track of it yourself; we have to do all these things. Most of our functions from society make the assumption that people make mistakes and there's someone to blame. It just says something about where we are as a society.

As a society, we just replay this whole thing over and over again. The professionals make the claim or sell into what the American public wants, which is, take care of it for me, give me a quick fix.

Correct. If it weren't for that, we'd have very few con artists in the world. But because people are greedy and they want the quick fix, it's a prime opportunity for con artists.

So, a bottom line seems to be to live out your dreams no matter whether it's trading stocks, or starting your own business or having a great relationship or whatever, "Take responsibility for your actions and learn enough about how to create it in a way that works."

Beliefs are simply useful. My particular belief is: We totally create our own life. And if you do that, then you have to take responsibility for what you create and figure out how you do it. To the extent that you start blaming others, you give up that power. So the first thing to do is take that power back.

I have a great story along this line. We had a school for traders, and we were going to recruit traders for a bank. The bank was going to give these recruits a million dollars. We ran ads and got two hundred applicants whom we interviewed over the phone. I put 20 of them into a seminar to decide who the ten best would be in our little school. And in the school was a fellow who was a quadriplegic. He'd been in a football accident, and he could barely use one hand, but he still functioned as a computer programmer. One of the things I was looking for was this trait of personal responsibility. And, of course, he was a total victim because he made the assumption that this accident happened to him, and now he was confined to the wheelchair, and so on and so forth. He didn't get into the school, and he thought about suing us for discrimination against people with disabilities. But fortunately, he got started in doing things like *A Course in Miracles*.

He eventually did some consulting with me. He said to me at that time that when he finally decided he was in some way responsible for his accident, it was probably the most freeing thing that ever happened to him. Because after that, he was in charge of his life. He started doing things proactively. He got a specially trained dog that could do a number of things for him, and trained the dog more, and his life just took off after that. But it took that one decision–that he created his whole life. People like to think, "Oh, I can't claim responsibility for something that's bad, how could that be?" But, when you do that, that's when you get control of your life.

I think you're right on the mark there. If something goes wrong, we want to look at who we can blame; it can't possibly be something we did. Or maybe it was an accident. But *we* really are the creators of our realities, and if we look at our thoughts and trace them back, we can see how we created what we have.

Absolutely.

Van, if we were to try to quantify this a bit, what is a monetary example of somebody who you worked with on their self-sabotaging behaviors and perhaps who was losing money in the market and then turned it around. Can you give us an example of what's possible and quantify it?

I'll give you one example. This was a floor trader that I worked with some time ago, but he was an options floor trader. His basic problem was that he would make a certain amount of money and then he'd stop. That was it, and it was enough to get by. But that was about all he could do. He'd make maybe $50,000 a year, and once he'd made that $50,000, he couldn't make any more. His whole issue had to do with being accepted by his father. He didn't want to make more money than his father did, and we did some parts exercises and a few things to overcome that.

He then had to face the stock market crash in 1987. The people who were hurt the worst were the option floor traders. He didn't participate in the crash, but afterwards, there were incredible opportunities and because he was now free, he earned in about two months more money than he'd made during the rest of his prior career.

When you say he was free, do you mean free of all those old beliefs?

Yes and free of the feelings. I think his father made about $50,000. He became free of, "I can't make anymore money than my dad." I think he made well over a million in a month or two.

Wow, so a major shift. All as a result, or mostly as a result of shifting...

One simple belief. The art is finding the belief.

The art of finding that core belief. And, that's the question that I would like to leave our readers with. What is at the core that's in the way? If you're not getting where you want to go, what is the core belief that's in the way?

Dr. Tharp, where can our readers go if they want to find more information about your home study course?

Our Web site is www.IITM.com. There, they can register for a free E-zine letter or a free copy of our newsletter. They can also call 1-800-385-4486. A simple place to start if they're interested in the market is my book, *Trade Your Way To Financial Freedom*. I also have a new book coming out called, *Safe Strategies For Financial Freedom*. And my Peak Performance Course is available through the Web site as well.

Great. I really appreciate everything you've said and how you applied your work to the stock market. I think if people will just listen to what you had to say today and learn to take responsibility for what they're creating in their lives, they can shift a lot of things.

I think so, too.

Three Key Success Principles Plus Coaching Questions and Action Steps

● ●

The Psychology of Living Out Your Dreams
Dr. Van K. Tharp

Key Success Principle #1:

Power-Shift from Victim to Creator of Your Life

Most people don't like to think of themselves as victims, but the truth is that we all play that part sometimes. Whenever you feel you are stuck in a rut–like there's no way out or like someone else is to blame–you are playing the role of victim.

When you depend on someone else to make decisions for you and you don't like the outcome, you may jump to blaming that person. Examples of people we tend to blame include stockbrokers, real estate agents, government officials, your boss, co-workers, etc.

When you find yourself blaming others or feeling sorry for yourself, it is time to shift your thinking from victim to creator.

We are all the creators of our own lives. Sometimes you may not like the results you get. Then it is time to look at how you contributed to this outcome and what you can do differently to get a better result as you go forward.

Coaching Questions:

1) Who are you pointing the finger at or blaming that you don't have the results you want?

2) What do you want to be different in that situation?

3) Where have you been relying on others to tell you what to do?

4) What do you need to learn to have a different outcome?

5) If you are taking responsibility for your life and still not getting where you want to go, ask yourself this question: What is at the core of me that is in the way?

You may want to get support in identifying and shifting this.

Call to Action:

1) Take responsibility for everything that is going on in your life, whether it is wanted or unwanted. Don't beat yourself up for it; just notice it and decide what you want to create differently.

Key Success Principle #2

Change Your Mind—Change Your Life: Reprogram Your Thoughts and Create What You Want

Let's take a look at the creation process and the principle that we are the creators of our own lives. It is actually a simple process. We create our lives through our thoughts, feelings and actions. When all three are in alignment, we are in the process of creation. So, if you want to make a change, and you believe you can do it, feel positive emotions around it, and take inspired steps toward making it happen, it will happen. If, at any point in that process, you don't believe you can do it or feel negative thoughts or emotions around it, then you are likely to slow down or even repel what you want from coming to you.

If you are frequently thinking about the fact that you don't have what you want, then you are focused on the lack of it, which is a negative thought. Thoughts are like magnets. Negative thoughts attract more negative thoughts and things associated with those thoughts. Positive thoughts attract more positive thoughts and things associated with those thoughts.

Coaching Questions:

1) What do you have in your life that you have been wanting?

2) What were the thoughts and beliefs you had prior to receiving those things?

3) What don't you have that you have been wanting?

4) What have been your thoughts and beliefs on this subject?

Call to Action:

1) Throughout the day, notice when you are thinking about what you don't want to happen. Shift to a positive thought about that subject that makes you feel just a little better about it. Don't expect to go from feeling very negative to very positive in one swoop. Think of things that feel slightly better and edge your thinking and energy up in increments.

   If you can't find a positive thought about that subject, shift your thoughts to something else that feels 100% positive. If you come back to the prior subject when you are feeling better, it will be easier to shift your thoughts about it.

Key Success Principle #3

Disarm That Sneaky Inner Saboteur

Dr. Tharp has found that even when we know what we need to do, we often don't do it out of fear of experiencing the emotions and other things that may come up as a result. I have found this to be true as well. I found many diversions along the way to keep me from actually completing this book. Luckily, I eventually realized what I was doing and made a pact not to take on any new projects until I completed it.

Fear of failure and fear of success are the two biggest internal fears that people often face. Most other fears such as fear of rejection fall underneath one of these major categories. As human beings, we will go to great lengths to avoid our fears. That is why so many ideas never get beyond being a great idea, or projects are started and never finished. It is easy to find reasons, excuses, other diversions or projects, create chaos, and sometimes even create emergencies to avoid these negative feelings or outcomes.

One of the most important things you can do is allow it to be okay to have these feelings. Then step back and notice what it is you do to get in your own way. When you have identified what you do, you can make a conscious decision to do it differently.

Coaching Questions:

1) When you think about moving forward with your dreams, what fears come up?

2) What are you afraid of experiencing?

3) What do you do to avoid experiencing that?

4) Does the fear keep you playing small or maybe not even playing at all?

5) Are you willing to allow it to be okay that you have those feelings?

6) Is there a particular success principle in this book that you know you should be following but you resist it?

Call to Action:

1) If you have been avoiding something because you are afraid, recommit to completing that project or attaining that dream.

2) Remove all distractions or other projects that you have taken on to avoid the one that is really important to you.

3) Say "no" to all other projects, until your most important one is complete.

4) Apply one or more success principles from this book in addition to the ones you were already using.

5) If at any point along the way, your fears or anxieties have you feeling paralyzed, there are many ways to deal with and move through them. One way is to find a coach to help you. There are also various non-traditional techniques such as Neuro Linguistic Programming (NLP) or energy techniques such as Emotional Freedom Technique (EFT) or BeSetFreeFast (BSFF). EFT and BSFF are the methods I use most often with my clients who have anxiety or emotional blocks. More information on these and other methods are provided in the Resource Section.

My Key Learnings from This Chapter:

1)

2)

3)

Chapter #9:
Summary

Summary

● ● ● ● ● ● ● ● ● ● ● ●

Common Themes

When I told people I was writing this book, everyone wanted to know the common themes among the people I interviewed. In other words, bottom line: What do all these successful people have in common?

The most prevalent themes among the people I interviewed were:

○ They *committed* to their dreams and were willing to do what it took to make them happen.

○ They got help–no one did it by himself or herself. They had coaches or mentors, took workshops, read books, and learned from those who had gone before them in some way.

○ They dealt with failure and moved on–it never stopped them for long.

○ They are passionate about what they do–no exceptions!

○ They utilized their natural talents and abilities and delegated the rest of the duties to people who specialized in them–people they could trust.

○ They continuously looked at how to expand their current capacity–to stretch themselves beyond the limits they previously knew.

○ They listened to their inner voice and acted on it rather than being run by what others thought they should do.

○ They made their dreams a priority and created their life around that rather than trying to fit their dreams into their life.

○ Many visualized themselves living out their dreams— sometimes for a long time—before they actually happened.

○ They learned how to minimize risk along the way. Some took bigger risks initially and then learned how to create a safety net along the way. Others, such as Tom Glavine, always had a back-up plan.

I think most people consider high achievers and entrepreneurs risk takers. That may be true to some degree but not to the extent people perceive it to be true. The more successful people typically learn how to create a safety net early on to minimize their risk. On the following pages, I have extracted examples from this book and from other real-life situations to illustrate various ways that people have minimized their risk.

Bonus Key Success Principle #1
• •

Create a Safety Net Before You Leap

There are lots of ways to create safety nets for your dreams and many types of safety nets. A safety net is simply a way to minimize risk while still moving forward in the direction of your dreams. The type of safety net you will need depends on your fears and concerns. You can create mental, financial and emotional safety nets.

Mental Safety Net:

The biggest key to minimizing risk is knowledge. The more you know about a subject, the more confidence you will have in your decisions and abilities related to that subject. If you don't feel as if you know enough to move forward on your dreams, make the first step to acquire more knowledge. The two questions to ask yourself are:

1) What do I need to know?

This could be anything from:

   Technical or how-to information: When taking on anything new, there will be a learning curve. Don't expect to know how to do something from the get-go. Be willing to learn how.
   Understanding terminology: There is terminology or lingo in every field. Learn it so you can play the game without feeling intimidated.

Pros and cons of a certain choice from people who are doing it:
Many people make the mistake of dreaming about a career that is
not based in reality. The best way to minimize risk here is to learn
the reality of what a career or option is really like. Shadow someone
for a day. You wouldn't buy a car without test driving it, would
you?

Skill set needed: Investigate what skills are most needed to be
successful. They might be different from what you think.

2)   Where can I get that information?

We live in the information age. Information is everywhere.
Resources include books, the Internet, television and videos,
workshops, continuing education, conversations with people who
have done what you want to do and coaches or mentors who
specialize in that area.

Financial Safety Net:

This is a huge area that gets in the way for people pursuing their
dreams. So often one hears people say, I'll do that when I win the
lottery... when I retire... when I am rich... There are many
approaches to creating a financial safety net.

If you are creating an entrepreneurial business where you work
out of your home, a good rule of thumb for taking the financial
leap is to have enough savings to live on for one year or more.
With that information in hand, you can start saving money on a
weekly or monthly basis to make that happen. Have it deducted
directly from your paycheck, so you are not tempted to spend it.

Another method is to create a bridge to your dreams. Perhaps
you want to go into business for yourself but you don't want to

wait until you have saved enough money. How could you get started sooner? One way might be to create your business on the side, so you are working on it in the evenings or weekends. Another way is to negotiate a four-day work week on your current job or create an interim job or income stream that gives you enough money to pay the bills and leaves you energy left over to move forward on your dream. I had one client who got clear about what she wanted to do and then intended for a severance package from her employer. Sure enough, she got it. This gave her the funds to go back to school and get a degree in her new chosen field.

Perhaps your dreams are larger and require start-up capital. Small business loans, venture capital, and business partners are all ways to finance your dreams. A formal business plan is usually needed in this case. You can get help with this from your local Small Business Development Center (SBDC).

While money is one of the biggest reasons that people give for not moving forward on their dreams, often there are other reasons behind it. If you are saying money is the drawback, brainstorm all the ways you could get the money and work out the money situation. Then notice if you are still reluctant to move forward. If so, you probably need to focus on the mental and emotional safety nets.

Emotional Safety Net:

Emotional reasons are things such as fear of failure, fear of success, fear of what others will think and limiting beliefs.

It is important to have a support team of people to call on when these fears come up. Otherwise, the fears can stop you dead in your tracks. Your team might consist of friends who are unconditionally supportive, a mentor, and/or a coach.

I highly recommend a structure for accountability such as working with a coach to support you as you move through your fears. Talking every week to a coach who acts as your cheerleader, consultant, brainstorm partner and confidant will help get you past those tough times and move forward in your dreams.

How the Experts Created a Safety Net:

Let's look at various examples of how some successful people have minimized risk or created safety nets for their dreams. I have included examples of people in this book as well as others whom you may or may not know.

From a very young age, Tom Glavine wanted to be a professional baseball player. He knew that the probability of getting to do that was small. Therefore, he kept up his grades so that he could go on to college if baseball did not pan out. He has continued the habit of having a back-up plan. Rather than spending all his money, he invests wisely and does not live an exorbitant lifestyle even though he probably could. He has money to live on in case of injury or unforeseen circumstances. He does not put all his eggs in one basket.

Jack Canfield and Mark Victor Hansen, co-authors of *Chicken Soup for the Soul,* the most widely sold book series in the country, got many rejections from publishers initially. Finally, a small publisher said he would print the book if they promised to buy 20,000 copies. They said yes. This may sound like a big risk. What most people don't know is that they basically had 20,000 promises in the form of coupons from people who said they would buy the book. So there was little risk in their moving ahead with this deal.

Stacy Allison takes physical risks in climbing mountains. But even she minimized her risk (and shortened her learning curve) by going on difficult climbs early in her career with people who had 10 years or more experience than she–people who were willing to teach her the tricks of the trade.

Loral Langemeier, a self-made millionaire, chose to learn from those more experienced than she was. She paid her own airfare to shadow and learn from the best in the business. In this way, she minimized the mistakes she would make from having to learn everything on her own.

Stephen Pierce took a risk by offering a program he had never taught before. He knew there was a demand for this program; however, because people offered to pay him for his knowledge before he ever created the program.

Ricky Frank, an affluent enamel artist, learned how to minimize risk as he progressed in his career. He got tired of his income being dependent on the opinion of a couple of people at juried art shows, so he hooked up with a wholesale distribution show and now has his jewelry in retail stores across the country. As the economy took a turn, Ricky learned other ways to minimize his risk. He now has a product line to suit low-, medium- and high-end budgets.

John Dessauer took a big risk initially when he quit his job. Since that time he has learned how to minimize risk by only falling in love with the numbers of a particular real estate deal, not the aesthetics. He also puts clauses in his sales contracts that free him from any obligation until he has conducted thorough due diligence on the property. He created a team of knowledgeable people that he can count on who have expertise in areas he does not. In his eyes, this is the biggest safety net he can establish.

Many people consider me a risk-taker because many years ago I left a six-figure corporate job to start my own business. What they don't know is that I stashed away my bonus checks and had money to live on for 1-2 years even if my business didn't make a dime. While it was still scary, my financial risk was minimal.

Coaching Questions:

1) In what area(s) do you need to create a safety net: Mental, Financial or Emotional?

2) What can you do to minimize your risk in these area(s) and still move forward in the direction of your dreams?

Call to Action:

1) Choose one area: (Mental, Financial or Emotional) that you would like to strengthen. List all the ways you could do that.

2) What can you do to minimize your risk in these area(s) and still move forward in the direction of your dreams?

3) Over the next week, take one step toward building a safety net in that area.

Bonus Key Success Principle #2
● ●

Be Like Gumby:
Stretch Beyond Your Comfort Zone

Living out your dreams will require you to stretch, get out of your comfort zone and try new things, even when you don't know how they will turn out. It is important to let go of your fear of the unknown and trust that you will be able to handle whatever happens. This doesn't mean jumping without a net; i.e., without any means of support or knowledge of what you are doing. It simply means to take small steps in the direction in which you want to go.

Often people only take on what they know they can do; i.e., they stay within their comfort zone. It is a natural tendency for people to want to stay within their comfort zone even if they are unhappy, simply because it is familiar and they perceive it is safe. I use the word "perceive" here because I have talked to many clients and prospective clients over the years who stayed in their jobs even though they were unhappy because they thought it was safe. The amount of layoffs in corporate America between the years 2000-2003 began to shake up that paradigm. I am proud to tell people that although the corporation I used to work for as VP, Human Resources is no longer in business, my small company is still prospering. Security is not found in a corporation or in anything external; it is found within ourselves.

How Our Experts Stretched:

Stacy Allison regularly stretches beyond her comfort zone. This plays a large role in her success. The first time Stacy scaled a rock, it was "very, very hard" for her. Later, she chose to climb a mountain that was a level 10 years beyond her experience. It is important to note that she went with people who had the experience and could guide her through the challenge.

Throughout her life, in climbing, speaking and writing, Stacy continued to take on challenges that were above and beyond what she knew she could do. In taking on these challenges, she increased her confidence in her abilities, pushed beyond what she knew herself capable of, and indeed became the first American woman to stand on top of Mt. Everest.

All of the people interviewed in this book stretched themselves time and time again. Stephen Pierce took on teaching a client how to invest, even though he had never done this before. Mary Youngblood asked to be the opening act on the PowWow Cruise. John Dessauer quit his job and invested in real estate for the first time. Loral Langemeier volunteered to work for someone for free in order to learn from them. Lisa McLeod quit a comfortable, prestigious corporate job to take a sales job and eventually to follow her passions. Tom Glavine left the familiarity of the Atlanta Braves to play for the N.Y Mets.

Coaching Questions:

1) Where in your career or personal life are you hanging out in your comfort zone even though you know that stretching beyond it would bring you closer to your dreams?

2) What thoughts or circumstances are keeping you there?

3) What are you resisting?

4) Who could you get to support you in moving forward? (Pick someone who will be unconditionally supportive.)

Call to Action:

1) Choose one area in which you would like to stretch your capacity. It could be physical, mental, emotional or spiritual.

2) Write down what it will provide for you to stretch there.

3) List all the things in this area you could do that would be a stretch; i.e., either it feels uncomfortable and you don't know how it will turn out or it's simply something you haven't done before. Pick one of them and take a small action on it this week.

Resources for Living Out Your Dreams

Books and Reports

Is Your Ladder Leaning Against the Wrong Wall? by Stacey Mayo, available at www.balancedliving.com

Special Report: From Starving Artist to Affluent Artist by Stacey Mayo, available soon at www.IGetPaidToDoThis.com

The Pathfinder by Nicholas Lore, Simon & Shuster, 1998

Making a Living Without a Job by Barbara Winter, Bantam, 1993

Excuse Me, Your Life is Waiting by Lynn Grabhorn, Hampton Roads, 2003

Spiritual Economics by Eric Butterworth, Unity Books, 2001

Creating Money by Sanaya Roman and Duane Packer, H.J. Kramer, 1988

Rich, Dad, Poor Dad: What the Rich Teach Their Kids About Money–That the Poor and Middle Class Do Not! by Robert Kiyosaki and Sharon L. Lechter, Warner Books, 2000

The One Minute Millionaire by Mark Victor Hansen and Robert G. Allen, Harmony, 2002

The Aladdin Factor: How to Ask for and Get Everything You Want by Jack Canfield and Mark Victor Hansen, Berkley, 1995

Multiple Streams of Income by Robert G. Allen, Wiley, 2004

Law of Attraction by Michael Losier, Michael Losier, 2003

Extreme Success: The 7-Part Program That Shows You How to Succeed Without Struggle by Rich Fettke, Simon & Shuster, 2002

The Wealthy Spirit: Daily Affirmations for Financial Stress Reduction by Chellie Campbell, Sourcebooks, 2002

Taming Your Gremlin: A Guide to Enjoying Yourself by Richard David Carson, Perennial Currents, 2003

Leadership and Self-Deception: Getting out of the Box by the Arbinger Institute, Berrett-Koehler, 2002

Audiotapes/CDs

The Law of Allowing and all audio sets, Abraham-Hicks, www.abraham-hicks.com, 2004

Career Testing

Rockport Career Test: In my opinion, this is the best career test out there. It is a timed test so it objectively measures what your aptitudes are, rather than asking you what you think you are good at or what you are interested in.

This is a great tool to use if you are unsure how to transfer your skills to another area, not sure you are in a job that is the best fit for you, or just want to be more productive in your career or business by better harnessing your strengths and delegating tasks related to your weaknesses. For more info, go to www.balancedliving.com/test

Free Downloadable Resources

These resources are available for readers of this book and clients of Center for Balanced Living at www.IGetPaidToDoThis.com/bookresources.

Values Assessment: Identify your inherited values, current values, and the values by which you choose to live your life from now on.

Gifts and Talents Questionnaire: Questionnaire designed to let you step into your greatness by seeing your natural gifts as others see them.

Top Ten Steps to Building Confidence: Free article

Getting Past the Oblocks: Free article

Resources for Finding a Coach

International Coach Federation: There are thousands of coaches around the world. Choosing one can seem daunting. The International Coach Federation's Coach Referral Service matches coaches with clients seeking their specific services and areas of expertise. Coaching is done very effectively over the phone, so location does not have to be a barrier, but if you have specific requirements, you can find coaches all over the world. For more info, visit www.coachfederation.org.

Center for Balanced Living: The coaches at the Center for Balanced Living have a diversity of backgrounds to support you in clarifying and living out your dreams, both career-wise and personally. Customized individual coaching is available. We are also creating coaching groups to support you in living the principles of this book. For more information, visit www.balancedliving.com or www.IGetPaidToDoThis.com.

Try Out a New Career While on Vacation

Vocation Vacations: Places vacationers in a dream job such as an innkeeper, brew master, winemaker, horse trainer, cheese maker, raceway manager, hunting and fishing guide, professional gardener, pastry chef or chocolatier. Available in various locations. Visit www.vocationvacations.com.

Getting Past the Fears and Obsticles

Emotional Freedom Technique (EFT): An effective energy-releasing technique that involves tapping on acupressure points while focusing on the block you have. Do this by yourself or with the help of a practitioner if you need help in identifying what's in your way. www.emofree.com

Be Set Free Fast (BSFF): Another effective energy technique that utilizes a cue word or phrase to release negative energy and blocks. www.bsff.com or www.prosperityplace.com

Dr. Tharp's Peak Performance Self-Study Program: This home study program contains five books by Dr. Tharp, and four audio cassettes.

These cassettes help guide you through exercises in the course on such topics as how you think when you make profits and lose money; stress reduction; programming yourself not to repeat your mistakes; and trading unemotionally. For more info, go to www.iitm.com.

Financing

Small Business Administration: www.sba.gov/financing

Small Business Development Center: www.sba.gov/sbdc

The MoneyTree Survey is a quarterly study of venture capital investment activity in the United States. As a collaboration between PricewaterhouseCoopers, Thomson Venture Economics and the National Venture Capital Association, it is the only industry-endorsed research of its kind. The MoneyTree Survey is the definitive source of information on emerging companies that receive financing and the venture capital firms that provide it. The study is a staple of the financial community, entrepreneurs, government policymakers, and the business press worldwide. Go to www.pwcmoneytree.com.

Private Equity Network: NVST is an Internet hub (or portal) for the worldwide private equity and finance community. The website provides online access to Venture Capital or Merger & Acquisition investment opportunities, professional journals, research databases and educational resources for professional training. Here, entrepreneurs and professionals in the private equity industry can find new deals, meet one another, access online business tools and learn more about their marketplace. Private equity is generally utilized to fund entrepreneurial businesses through venture capital and mergers and acquisitions. NVST Inc gives the entire industry instant access to deals, financing resources, online business tools and education. www.nvst.com/pnvHome.asp

Small Business Resources on the Intrenet

www.allbusiness.com: Small business resources to help you start, manage, and develop your business. Business plans, marketing tips, computer knowledge, hiring strategies, business loans, legal advice, and more.

www.entrepreneur.com: Information on starting and growing a small business including downloadable forms and tools.

www.morebusiness.com: Sample business plans, sample contracts, sample marketing plans, business loans, employee manuals.

www.workingsolo.com: The information source for independent entrepreneurs and companies serving the SOHO (small office/ home office with fewer than 20 employees) market.

www.startupjournal.com: The Wall Street Journal Center for Entrepreneurs.

www.bplans.com: Business plan software and free sample business plans.

Web Sites of the Cast of this Book

Stacy Allison   www.beyondthelimits.com

Mary Youngblood   www.maryyoungblood.com

Stephen Pierce   www.impulsiveprofits.com

Loral Langemeier   www.liveoutloud.com
www.wealthdiva.com

John Dessauer   www.thedessauergroup.com

Lisa Earle McLeod   www.forgetperfect.com

Dr. Van K. Tharp   www.iitm.com

About the Author

A well-known coach with a wide following, Stacey Mayo, a.k.a. "The Dream Queen," was a pioneer in the now-booming coaching industry. Stacey established the Center for Balanced Living in 1995 as a vehicle to carry out her life's work. As director of the Center, she and a team of powerful coaches have assisted thousands of people across the nation in living out their dreams with amazing results.

Stacey was profiled on television in the CBS Evening News segment, "Confident Women." She has also appeared on the Atlanta Business Chronicle Reports. She has been featured a number of times in the Atlanta Journal-Constitution, including the piece, "Midlife," which engages women in considering how they can stop deferring their dreams.

A leader in the coaching community and former program chair for the International Coaching Federation (ICF), Stacey has developed and led hundreds of successful training and coaching programs to rave reviews. She is a popular public speaker and author of *Is Your Ladder Leaning Against the Wrong Wall?*

Stacey is a Master Certified Coach, a member of the International Coaching Federation, a graduate of Coach University, and is certified as a career coach through Rockport Institute. She received a B.S. Business from Tulane University.

Stacey loves to help people live out their dreams and expand their success by getting out of their own way, balancing their personal and business lives, creating wealth while doing something they love and shouting from the rooftop, *"I Can't Believe I Get Paid To Do This!"*

Stacey lives with her husband and two golden retrievers, LB (Lover Boy) and Georgia, in a suburb of Atlanta.

For her free online newsletter, Living Out Your Dreams, or more information about her services, visit www.balancedliving.com and www.IGetPaidToDoThis.com.